TRADING THE
SHAREMARKET
THE ASX WAY

Wrightbooks

First published 2004 by Wrightbooks
an imprint of John Wiley & Sons Australia, Ltd
33 Park Road, Milton, Qld 4064
Offices also in Sydney and Melbourne

Typeset in Berkeley LT 11.2/14.3 pt

© The Australian Stock Exchange 2004

National Library of Australia
Cataloguing-in-Publication data:

Trading the sharemarket - the ASX way
Includes index

ISBN 0 7314 0197 2

1. Stocks - Australia. 2. Investments - Australia.
3. Portfolio management - Australia. 4. Asset allocation - Australia.
5. Retirement income - Australia. I. Australian Stock Exchange
II. Title : Trading the sharemarket - the ASX way.

332.60994

Some material included in this publication has been previously published as ASX course notes.

Cover design by Rob Cowpe

Cover photo © Australian Stock Exchange Limited. Used with permission.

Printed in Australia by Griffin Press

10 9 8 7 6 5 4 3 2 1

Disclaimer

The material in this publication is of the nature of general comment only, and neither purports nor intends to be advice. Readers should not act on the basis of any matter in this publication without considering (and if appropriate taking) professional advice with due regard to their own particular circumstances. The ASX and publisher expressly disclaim all and any liability to any person, whether a purchaser of this publication or not, in respect of anything and of the consequences of anything done or omitted to be done by any such person in reliance, whether in whole or part, upon the whole or any part of the contents of this publication.

Contents

About the *ASX way* series

These days many people claim to be investment educators or to have the secret to making a million. But there is really no secret — most successful investing is based on careful research and disciplined investing.

With so many people saying so many different things about investing, where do people go for sound, practical and trustworthy investment education? The Australian Stock Exchange (ASX) has been offering practical, easy-to-understand education since the exchange was formed in 1987. Before that, stock exchanges in capital cities around the country were often the only place to go to learn about investing in the sharemarket. Demand has grown considerably since then, with more than 160,000 Australians learning about investing through ASX education channels in 2003.

Investment education is not just for adults — young Australians are getting more involved much earlier these days, particularly by playing the ASX sharemarket game. Over half the high schools in the country now have students competing in the games, while also learning about the risks and the rewards of investing in the sharemarket.

The *ASX way* series of investment books published by Wrightbooks gives investors the benefits of the Stock Exchange's years of experience and authority, packed into three easy-to-follow investment books. The *ASX way* series of books allows people to start from scratch, building their expertise and their confidence as they work through each book.

The first book in the series, *Starting out in shares – the ASX way*, covers the fundamentals. It assumes no prior knowledge and gives people the knowledge that is required before they can do further reading. The book identifies what share investment is all about — not only in terms of performance, but also in terms of how the share investment category fits in with broader portfolios. Consideration is given to finding appropriate shares for the individual investor by introducing common methods of sharemarket analysis as well as teaching appropriate methods of keeping track of the investment over time. The aim of this introductory volume is to provide new investors with the solid fundamental grounding that is common to all successful investors. By utilising this strong foundation, investors will be taking the first steps to expanding their knowledge and understanding of the sharemarket.

Book two, *Trading the sharemarket — the ASX way*, is all about helping people who are at the next stage. They have done their preparation and now they want to trade some shares. The book goes into the sorts of things people need to think about, the different types of trading strategies that can be used and how they should develop a plan for their own trading. Consideration is also given to the management of the investor's portfolio.

Trading options — the ASX way is book three. It covers the exchange-traded options market. At ASX we say options are clever products for clever investors. Many people think these products are only for professionals but most options investors are what we call 'retail investors'. Individual shareholders are using options to make money in rising and falling markets, and to earn extra income on their share portfolios. The third book in the *ASX way* series explains how you can also use options for these purposes. As with all the books in the series, *Trading options — the ASX way* explains the risk as well as the opportunities.

Foreword

This is the second book in the *ASX way* series and it builds on the material from the first book, *Starting out in shares — the ASX way*. This book is designed to help those who want to have more control over their investments.

Learning about investment in the sharemarket is an ongoing process for any investor. Any attempt to become a successful investor in a single step will invariably prove to be an exercise in futility. Successful investing is all about having a grasp of vital concepts which should be applied sensibly, as well as having the ability to learn from past experiences. Regardless of how well structured your initial investment plan is, it should change over time as your experiences teach you new lessons about how to approach different situations in the sharemarket.

Over the past few years there has been an explosion of people who want to have direct control of their share investments. The growth in self-managed superannuation has been nothing short of astounding. The major skill needed by those using an SMSF is the ability to select investments that suit their needs. In many cases, investors are keen to take control of their own superannuation but are left in a position where they lack the ability to prudently select their own investments. As you can imagine, this may result in substantial damage to their long-term portfolio.

Trading in shares, at its most basic, involves buying when you believe the price is low and selling when you believe the price is high. Although this could not sound easier, in reality it is quite hard. Firstly, cheap and expensive are relative terms — what is cheap for me may be expensive for you. Also, the time frame of the trader is a vital ingredient. The longer you are invested in a company the greater the return should be. This is not to say that short-term gains are not possible — they are.

In this book, we start to explain and use the tools that traders use to help make decisions. Traders are usually exponents of fundamental or technical analysis. Neither is better than the other, so we cover the basics of both. We will also begin to show you the importance of a plan. Having a plan is vital — it tells you what and when to buy and sell. Sticking to your plan is also necessary. In my frequent conversations with investors, I find that people can quickly become frustrated in their efforts to develop their trading plan. Many new investors look to recognised investment professionals to provide them with the one secret that will lead them to certain wealth. While many of these experts will be themselves excellent share investors, it is impossible for them to pass their experience on to you in one simple step. If you are able to keep your learning expectations reasonable and your time frame realistic, you will see much greater long-term success.

What I see across all investors is that the people who are passionate about the sharemarket frequently do very well. These are the people who long ago realised that there were no short cuts and who aren't afraid to work hard for the success that they desire. There is potential to make fantastic long-term wealth through investment in the sharemarket. With this in mind, realise that the more you can learn about the market, the better your results will be. Take on knowledge in all its forms —from books and seminars, and family and friends. The more pieces of wisdom you can store away the more effective an investor you will be. Build your plan and amend it as necessary. Be realistic in expectations of returns and above all of yourself. Don't be disheartened by setbacks and focus on your goals no matter what they may be.

Paul Dolan
Head of Investor Education
Australian Stock Exchange
Sydney, NSW

Part I
Successful share trading

Trading the sharemarket — the ASX way has been written for share investors who already have some understanding of how the stock market works. More importantly, it is for people who realise that investing in shares and managing an active portfolio can often bring better returns than investing in other asset classes, and who want to know how to do so more effectively.

The first part of this book looks at the benefits of adopting a share trading strategy. It considers stock selection methods, managing a portfolio, trading, and allocating and reviewing your investments. The main focus of Part I is using an investment, or long-term, account — although the use of a speculating, or short-term, account will also be looked at in Chapter 12.

1 Keys to investing success

The importance of strategy

If you are going to invest in shares directly, you need to come up with your own strategy. Your share trading strategy should reflect your own circumstances, responsibilities and tolerance for risk. Relying on the advice of others may prove folly and so in this book we encourage an independent approach. While you will certainly need to seek professional advice from time to time, an informed investor will more easily be able to evaluate and respond effectively to this advice.

A strategy can be thought of as simply a set of rules or guidelines that are adopted consistently over time. The strategy is often more important than the investments that are made through the implementation of that strategy.

The strategy is always the focal point and adhering to the strategy becomes the most important objective. Having a strategy, however, does not preclude you from losses and it is during periods of adversity that your ability to stick to your strategy will be tested.

This chapter provides some insights into the mindset required to follow the strategy that you have adopted. The key to adopting the right mindset lies in understanding how important time (especially a long-term perspective), consistency and discipline, and patience are to successful investing. Such an understanding will help you maintain an appropriate disregard for short-term volatility and take a more objective, consistently rational, approach to wealth creation.

You will also see how by having your own focused strategy you can diversify your investments more effectively — with the objective of improving overall returns, rather than simply diversifying for its own sake.

Time

Volatility

Volatility is a measure of the amount of fluctuation in price of the underlying security calculated using the standard deviation of average daily price change.

Most inexperienced investors expect too much too soon — they are attracted to the idea of making a fast buck. For this reason, short-term price volatility can be seen as the enemy. While positive volatility may encourage the belief that it really is possible to make $1 million overnight, negative volatility may result in losses and impatience, and increase the temptation to deviate from a strategy.

A long-term view on the stock market is important as it allows enough time for significant improvements in financial circumstances to accrue. Even if you are trading some of your portfolio regularly in a short-term time frame, your overall goal must generally be a long-term one.

A complete understanding of the rewards and the risks is required before a long-term view can be accepted and adopted. Importantly, some speculation is acceptable. Indeed, for many, the fun associated with making an educated bet is enough to warrant the speculative purchase of a particular share. However, while limited speculation with the right tools and risk management techniques can be fun and possibly profitable, it should *not* dominate an investor's portfolio — rather it should only be a small part of it. This way, spectacular losses need not be detrimental to the long-term wealth creation goals set in place at the inception of the strategy.

Speculation

Speculation is the taking of relatively large risks in the expectation of making relatively large gains in the short term.

Later in this book, we will examine methods for both long-term investing and short-term speculating.

Time and perceptions of volatility

Let's look further at volatility over the long term. For the 50 calendar years to December 2000, returns provided by the ASX All Ordinaries Accumulation Index have averaged 13.1 per cent per annum. These returns, however, do not give a complete picture of the investing environment nor the impact on an investor's emotions.

It is very easy, and indeed somewhat comforting, to look back over the last decade or two or even more and calculate the average annual rate of growth of the sharemarket. Such an exercise, however, almost completely masks the difficult part of investing in shares — responding responsibly to the daily ups and downs in the sharemarket that are examined, analysed and dissected by the media and numerous commentators and gurus.

Perhaps it is prudent to look at an analogy using the most successful investment for many Australians — the family home. When buying a house, a long-term investment is often being made. Indeed, given the unpleasant experience of moving house and the costs associated with the transaction, the homeowner may never want to move again! While homeowners will boast about house price increases and the shrewdness of their property investment, they will not move. Perhaps more relevant is that during periods when house prices decline, homeowners don't immediately put their home on the market (unless they are forced to).

What if the live prices of homes were displayed on screens daily and then reported in the financial media each night? Imagine a newsreader reporting the following:

Inner-west house prices fell for the fourth consecutive day as fears of a street widening saw owners selling and moving east. Financial commentator Wayne Fluff from Fluff Investments said, 'Inner-west house prices have peaked. There is a high degree of uncertainty and traders are looking to the next round of RBA board meetings to determine the medium-term direction. Most professionals are now sitting on cash in expectation of further weakness and waiting for bargains in the inner-west'.

In the north, prices have stabilised again after a vicious slide sent prices into a tailspin. Owners and traders sold

*property heavily amid fears the refusal by council to allow
a new shopping centre would see tourist numbers and
revenues in the region decline.*

*Inner-west properties dropped 1.2 per cent, northern
suburbs' values were down 2 per cent, the east was firm
on expectations that views facing towards the sun would
continue to demand a premium. The big surprise,
however, has been the jump overnight in the southern
suburbs prices. Three- and four-bedroom homes doubled
amid talk professionals were rotating from the northern
sector to the south. Meanwhile outer suburbs' prices
were steady and analysts believe much of the effect from
the forthcoming ESP tax has now been factored in. The
Sydney medium house index fell slightly on the day to
close at 245,314. And that's all from the finance desk.*

As ridiculous as it sounds, this is happening every day in
the sharemarket.

Why do many Australians perceive that their home is
the best investment they can make? Why do they assume it
is a long-term investment and are happy to ride out any
short-term fluctuations? We would suggest it's because
property prices are not advertised as widely and as often as
share prices, nor are they subject to the short-term
psychological influences that can change the prices of
individual listed shares.

Volatility is a good thing. Positive volatility causes
prices to rise, increasing the value of the investments and
the wealth of the investor. Negative volatility can also be
viewed positively if it is seen as an opportunity to purchase
good quality businesses at lower prices. However, most
investors see volatility as a dangerous thing. We would like
you to reconsider the way you view volatility and, as you
will see shortly, think about how volatility actually proves
to be less of a concern the longer you invest.

Compounding

Compounding is a process whereby the value of an investment or series of investments increases exponentially over time through profits from the investing being reinvested and so attracting more growth and profits.

Better returns over time

Time is the undisputed champion for the investor. It is time
alone that can stop you having to work for your money
and start your money working for you. Once you start
making money, the gains can increase exponentially as

previous gains attract more. The process is called compounding and all it needs to work is time.

For most investors, a single asset class will rarely be their only investment choice over time. History has shown that no single asset class will generate superior returns in excess of other asset classes perpetually.

Figure 1.1: Comparative pre-tax investment returns 1992–2004

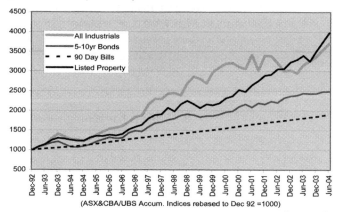

(ASX&CBA/UBS Accum. Indices rebased to Dec 92 =1000)

Source: ASX

In general terms, investors would expect to receive lower, but at the same time less volatile returns from their fixed-interest investments such as bonds. It should be kept in mind though that at times over the last 20 years, long-term bonds have periodically outperformed growth assets such as shares and property when the value of these assets has been widely depressed.

When you see the returns of shares presented in graphical or tabular form, it is important that you realise the returns you see will be representative of a major index and not individual shares. Your individual portfolio may return results that are quite different from those provided by the major indices. On some occasions, your portfolio may do better than a particular index, and at other times it may do worse. Your goal of course is to outperform the index wherever possible.

Indices
In addition to the All Ordinaries and accumulation indices, there are a number of other indices representing smaller or more specific sectors of the sharemarket.

The chart above clearly shows that although you can expect periods of downward movement, as your time horizon extends, overall performance of shares improves.

Lower volatility over time

Looking at performance without assessing risk, however, is dangerous — it is important to also examine whether the risk is higher or lower with the passing of time. We will see that not only does investing for longer periods usually result in better performance but also lower volatility.

Figure 1.2, below, displays an important observation in share investment — that is, generally speaking, the longer you invest, the lower your volatility of returns.

Figure 1.2: Relationship between time in the market and volatility

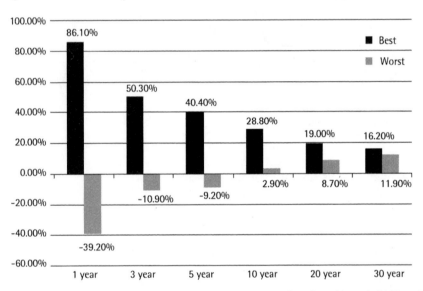

Data derived from: AndexCharts Pty Ltd

As you can see from Figure 1.2, investing for one year could see your returns vary between a loss of 40 per cent and a gain of nearly 90 per cent. Investing for 20 years results in the range of annualised return narrowing to between a gain of 9 per cent at worst and 20 per cent at best. Volatility, it would seem, is less of a concern for the long-term investor.

Dividends and time

There is another measure which shows the stock market is not as volatile as you may think — dividends.

As well as increases and decreases in the value of the stock you hold, additional income is generated by dividends. Figure 1.3, below, takes National Australia Bank (NAB) as an example and shows that since the early 1990s dividends per share (DPS) have steadily increased. Indeed, there has not been a decline in the dividend per share for this company for over a decade. The share price, however, is far from consistent in the market's evaluation of the merits of NAB's business. While in 1999 the share price fell 34 per cent, from around $30 to around $20, the dividends paid continued to increase.

Figure 1.3: NAB share price and dividends over 10 years to 2004

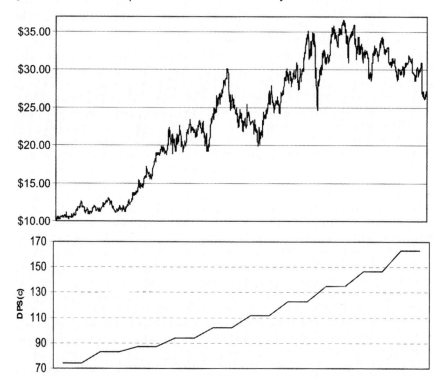

Looking at the market this way is a little like looking at the property market from the perspective of rents received. Good quality properties will rarely see weekly rents decline significantly. This perspective may help you in your quest to stick with a long-term approach to investing.

Rates of return and time

Share traders will not just accept the returns of the major index. Their objective is to attempt to outperform the index using approaches that have been tested previously by fund managers and wealthy private investors around the globe. One of the simplest ways to beat the market, however, is to wait for opportunities that provide cheaper investment entry points and be able to hold these investments. This approach in itself can significantly alter the long-term returns for an investor.

Take the case of an investor who in 2004 invested $100,000 in a particular share, paying $8 a share that in 15 years is expected to trade at $45. The investor's annualised rate of return if the shares reach $45 would be 12.2 per cent. Now suppose the investor waited for a situation that caused the shares to fall by 50 per cent to $4 and decided to invest the $100,000 to purchase the shares at this new level. If the shares eventually do trade at $45 in 15 years, the annualised return to the investor would be approximately 17.5 per cent.

While the difference of 5 per cent may not seem significant, the end results displayed in Figure 1.4, opposite, show a substantial disparity.

Figure 1.4 reveals the startling contrast in end results for an investor who accumulates returns at a rate of 17.5 per cent per year for 15 years and an investor who accumulates returns at 12.5 per cent over the same period. Simply buying at a cheaper price — and, hence, being able to buy a greater number of shares — has resulted in $100,000 growing to more than $1.3 million for the first situation compared to just over $630,000 for the second. Small increases in performance when compounded over time significantly improve the results. Don't forget this — every extra percentage point counts.

Later we will explore the various techniques investors can use to attempt to outperform the market index and predict potential movements in share prices. For now, however, it is essential you understand that investing in the sharemarket is generally a long-term activity.

Figure 1.4: Benefit of a cheaper entry price

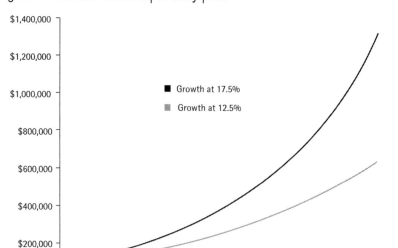

Consistency and discipline

The subject of consistency and discipline is perhaps more important when discussing financial matters than in many other fields. Failing to act in a disciplined and rigorous way, and to do so consistently over time, can result in poor performance. It is as simple as that. Consistency and discipline are the two most important keys to financial markets success.

As James O'Shaugnessey wrote in the investment classic *What works on Wall Street*:

> *Finding exploitable investment opportunities does not mean it's easy to make money. To do so requires the ability to consistently, patiently and slavishly stick with a strategy, even when it's performing poorly relative to other methods. Few are capable of such action.*

Before we elaborate on consistency and discipline as the two keys to market success, we need to understand the market itself.

The efficient market

The efficient market theory helps explain why many individual and professional investors fail to beat the market. Indeed, it claims that there is no possibility, except by chance, that any person or group can outperform the market, and certainly no chance that the same person or group could consistently do so. The problem, however, with the efficient market hypothesis is that it makes the assumption that all investors act rationally and that all information is processed correctly — that is, that no one makes mistakes.

Any share traders or investors can make the following observation — traders don't act rationally. Do you think it was rational valuation analysis that saw investors in the United States during the tech boom pay 500 times earnings per share for Yahoo or 300 times earnings for AOL? Or were these movements motivated by greed? In most cases, rational investing is a rare quality — although when harnessed it can provide excellent rewards.

Many active investors don't process information correctly or quickly. An announcement that is positive for a company may see its price quickly pushed higher by early buyers. A week later, other traders may only just be hearing the news. If they act on that information, it may provide nothing more than an opportunity for the early buyers to sell.

Esteemed academics may successfully argue that the markets are efficient and many PhDs and MBAs have been written on the topic. Opponents of these arguments contend that at the very least it would be wrong to conclude markets are efficient all the time.

While efficient market theory is cited as the reason many professional investors fail to beat the market over time, other reasons are that professional managers change jobs, get bored or simply try different ideas when their method is not performing satisfactorily. Rational consistency, on the other hand, is the hallmark of all of the world's best investors.

Earnings per share

Earnings per share is the net profit for ordinary shares divided by the number of ordinary shares on issue.

A consistent approach

Empirical evidence supports the contention that consistency is an important key to successful wealth creation. The biggest and best names in the stock market, and some of the wealthiest individuals in the world, are experts at being consistent. Warren Buffett and Peter Lynch are two world-famous fund managers who have developed excellent models for stock selection. While every investor clamours to find out what tools they use, the most important factor — consistency — is rarely spoken about.

Warren Buffett is perhaps the best example of the consistent investor. For decades his Berkshire Hathaway shareholders have enjoyed returns of around 22 per cent per annum.[1] If this rate of return doesn't impress you, think about it this way — $100,000 invested with Buffett in 1974 would have been worth almost $41 million by 2003.

At the height of the technology boom in 1999, Buffett's Berkshire Hathaway was targeted by the financial media and the financial press for failing to take advantage of the astronomical prices being paid for technology stocks. As we have already noted, US companies were trading at up to 500 times earnings per share. In 1999, 279 internet companies listed in the United States and their average first day gain was 90 per cent. At the time, the media, the analysts and investors were lured into believing that the bubble would never burst.

At this point it might pay to take a side step and look at some wisdom from the father of security analysis, Benjamin Graham:

One of the striking features of the past five years has been the domination of the financial scene by purely psychological elements. In previous bull markets, the rise in stock prices remained in fairly close relationship with the improvement in business during the greater part of the cycle; it was only in the invariably short-lived culminating phase that quotations were forced to disproportionate heights by the unbridled optimism of the speculative contingent. But in the [most recent] cycle this

---

1   Source: Berkshire Hathaway annual report 2003.

*'culminating phase' lasted for years instead of months,
and it drew its support not from a group of speculators
but from the entire financial community. The 'new era'
doctrine...was at bottom only a means of rationalising
under the title of 'investment' the well-nigh universal
capitulation to the gambling fever.* [2]

Graham goes onto argue that the rise of psychological elements in financial markets is due to the increase in importance given to intangible factors such as goodwill and expected earnings power. As the standards used to measure such factors are subjective, the value given to them, and hence the value built into the share price, can vary greatly depending on the prevailing market sentiment.

This is clearly an insightful analysis of a boom. There doesn't seem to be much remarkable about this observation other than it was written in 1934. It was based on the boom that occurred just before the great depression. It's incredible that the boom of 1987 and the boom in technology stocks that occurred in 1999 can be summarised in exactly the same way. It would seem that each boom to a high degree resembles past booms. And every boom that has ever been has bust.

During the tech boom, while the market commentators seemed to forget this and once again pronounced 'this time is different' and 'this is a new era', Buffett was acutely aware of the bubble forming. Nevertheless, many told Buffett that he should retire, that he didn't understand the 'new economy' and that the 0.5 per cent return on his fund in 1999 was confirmation that his strategies no longer worked.

Why Buffett's strategy did not allow him to invest in internet or tech stocks is discussed in Chapter 4.

As Buffett's strategy did not allow him to invest in internet or tech stocks, he did not enjoy the exponential returns technology stocks were providing to more aggressive growth managers — at one point shares in his Berkshire Hathaway fund were down 30 per cent from $US65,000 per share to less than $US45,000 per share.

Despite media articles and special newspaper lift-outs entitled 'The end of the old world economy' further

---

2   Source: Benjamin Graham & David Dodd, *Security analysis*, McGrawHill Book Company Inc, 1934.

reinforcing the idea that old economy company shares were dead and high-tech shares were the way of the future, Warren Buffett did not succumb to the mounting pressure to change his strategy.

In April 2000, when the Nasdaq took its first dive and the subsequent sell off was labelled 'the tech wreck' by the media, the spotlight turned back to Buffett. The Berkshire Hathaway share price began to recover strongly and Buffett was asked to explain how he did it and what his secret was.

His answer was that there is no secret. All he did was act consistently. It is difficult to stick to a plan that is apparently not working. It is even more difficult when the world's financial media are telling you that you're wrong. However, a plan should have financial targets in place to tell you when to reduce your activity or reassess your plan. Until those targets are met, it's generally beneficial to stick to the plan.

Perversely, following any methodology consistently means that you *will* go through periods of poor performance — or what we refer to as 'drawdown'. It is extremely difficult to continue trading a method that is not working well — particularly when someone you know is enjoying a solid period of growth at the same time. Most people will be tempted to change their method or switch to a new method entirely. Don't. Provided you have thoroughly researched your technique, you should be aware of previous periods where the technique did not perform exceptionally well. What you are experiencing now may simply be normal in terms of the strategy's behaviour.

Drawdown
Drawdown is the period during which the equity in your account is falling because you have entered into a period of losses.

Unfortunately, sticking to the plan is easier said than done. As humans, we find it difficult to separate ourselves from the exciting story of a single stock. Very rarely do we favour the evidence or a large number of similar cases. We tend to be more interested in this story than in that class of companies or class of shares. If the story of a single company is sufficiently compelling, we may wager a bet on it even if the statistics suggest that historically following such a story is folly.

Discipline

A lack of consistency will result in underperformance. Following the recommendations of newsletters, or of television personalities, magazines or even astrology *may* be effective. However, the only way to determine if those methods *are* effective is to follow them rigorously. And perhaps that is the most important advantage of a consistent approach: the ability to objectively assess whether a tipster, newsletter or television host is actually any good.

Consider a casino. Why do they seem to win? Simple — they play games and impose rules that put mathematical expectation in their favour. They play the same games consistently, meaning the longer you play, the more likely they will win. You couldn't establish a casino business and borrow millions of dollars to fund that business if you set up the games to give the gambler an advantage.

For most share traders their experience in the markets can be a little like an evening at the casino. Without a strategy, you are gambling. With a strategy but not the discipline to consistently adhere to it, you are also gambling. However, while with a strategy and the discipline to consistently adhere to it you may still be gambling, you more closely resemble the casino. The odds, so to speak, are more likely to be in your favour. You need to have a competitive advantage and you need to keep playing that advantage over a long time.

Having a strategy that is applied consistently frees the investor from the emotions involved in the investing process and releases that individual to discover the benefits of a tested approach applied in a disciplined way, over an extended period of time, regardless of market circumstances.

Patience

Part of a disciplined approach, and an important aspect in investing and trading, is patience. It takes time for the market to recognise what you may already have realised about a company's shares. It takes time for the company to generate profits and pay those out to shareholders. It takes time to run a business in such a way that it produces positive surprises for the market. So if it takes time for all these good things to happen, why is it we can't wait for this time to pass?

A remark you will hear often (or may have even said yourself) goes along the lines of, 'These shares are for the long term'.

How many times have you purchased shares and made this remark? Many investors make exactly the same remark every day and yet, as soon as the stock starts to fall, they begin to sell out in a panic. Why? The 'long term' for the investor in this share may have begun just four weeks ago! So why has his or her sentiment changed now?

A lack of patience and fear are the culprits. We lack the patience to ride out the storm and we fear that things may never improve. Both are emotional responses when none is required. For many investors, selling out will be justified by explaining that the shares will be repurchased at a lower price. Rarely, if ever, are the shares repurchased at the lower price because the news that is pushing the price lower is bad. The investor will wait until things improve and the improvement is confirmed in the press. By this stage, the price of the shares is invariably higher than the price at which the shares were sold.

Even in short-term trading, patience is a key to success. The trader must be comfortable allowing prices to trend for long enough that a substantial profit accrues. During a period or string of losing trades, the trader must be patient and continue to follow his or her plan through to the next winning trade.

A healthy dollop of patience once a strategy has been researched, adopted and implemented is essential to success.

Further benefits of having a strategy to your share trading is discussed in the next chapter.

Choosing appropriate asset allocation

Within your stock selection strategy, once you have determined your risk profile, current financial position, your investment objectives, time frame and your liquidity requirements, you need to work out what proportion of your total capital you should invest in shares, property, fixed interest and cash. This is called asset allocation.

Each sector should be weighted in accordance with economic conditions and investment prospects. This helps to reduce volatility and risk in your portfolio. Of equal importance is the need to achieve a balance between income and growth while minimising your taxation liability.

If your income requirement is high, you should consider investing in fixed interest, cash and listed property trusts. You should also consider reducing your exposure to the international share sector and increasing your exposure to the Australian shares which pay higher dividends, paying due regard to whether they are fully franked dividends.

If you require growth rather than income, a lesser emphasis should be given to fixed interest and property, in favour of achieving greater exposure from both Australian and international shares.

For example, a retired married couple with a portfolio of $400,000 may not be too concerned if their portfolio falls in value by 10 per cent, providing they continue to receive an after-tax income of $25,000 per annum without having to draw down (or sell) assets to do so.

If, however, their portfolio contains several speculative investments which have not been successful, and they have lost assets as well as investment income, the portfolio may be outside their risk parameters.

Your risk/reward profile

Every investor has a different risk/reward profile. Taking the time to identify your own risk/reward profile will help you choose the best investments for your needs. The three most common types are outlined below.

The cautious investor

Cautious investors seek better than basic returns, but insist that the risk must still be low. Typically older investors, they seek to protect wealth that they have accumulated. They may be prepared to consider growth investments that are less aggressive.

The prudent investor

Prudent investors want a balanced portfolio to work towards medium- to long-term financial goals. They require an investment strategy that will cope with the effects of tax and inflation. Calculated risks aimed at achieving greater returns, in the form of both income and growth, are acceptable to them.

The aggressive investor

Aggressive investors are prepared to take greater risks in pursuit of potentially higher long-term and short-term gains. They may take on a higher level of gearing and business risk. However, it still will not be a total win/lose portfolio.

Allocating assets according to your risk/reward profile

Possible proportions for asset allocation depending on your attitude to risk are set out below. You should, however, obtain professional advice from a financial adviser.

The asset split for a cautious investor may be:

- Australian cash 25 per cent
- Australian fixed interest 40 per cent
- Australian shares 15 per cent
- Australian property 10 per cent
- overseas shares 10 per cent.

Asset allocation for a prudent investor may be:

- Australian cash 20 per cent
- Australian fixed interest 30 per cent
- Australian shares 25 per cent
- Australian property 10 per cent
- overseas shares 15 per cent.

For the aggressive investor, asset allocation may be:

- Australian cash 5 per cent
- Australian fixed interest 10 per cent
- Australian shares 45 per cent
- Australian property 15 per cent
- overseas shares 25 per cent.

For further discussion on the features of asset classes other than shares, see Chapter 14.

Aggressive investors tend to view risk as an opportunity rather than a threat. They are driven by the potential for capital gain. Most of them are prepared to borrow money to invest, and have done so from time to time. In terms of composition, their portfolios are very growth-oriented.

What do the professionals do?

The asset allocation practices of professional fund managers can often provide a useful investment guide. For example, when investing for a self-managed superannuation fund, investors may find it useful to follow a strategy similar to that used by large, pooled superannuation funds.

These large funds generally have a strong bias toward equities, particularly Australian equities and fixed-interest investments. This is because, firstly, their investment horizon is typically long term, meaning they use shares to weight their investments towards asset classes which perform better over time. Secondly, they usually have a significant amount of fixed-interest investments from which they can earn income and which they can trade to make capital profits. Finally, as superannuation funds pay only 15 per cent tax, franking credits can be used to offset taxation liabilities relating to other income, particularly fixed-interest income and tax on contributions to the fund.

The strategic asset allocation for a typical balanced fund might be as shown in Table 1.1, opposite.

Table 1.1: Typical asset allocation for a balanced fund

Asset class	Strategic asset allocation %	Asset range %
Australian shares	40	20-70
International shares	15	5-30
Australian bonds	10	0-30
International bonds	5	0-15
Property	15	10-30
Cash	15	5-40

Deciding on the amount of your overall funds you are going to allocate to share investment is an important part of your stock selection strategy and a key to investment success.

The benefits of having a strategy

After reading the first chapter, you should be starting to realise the importance of having a strategy. A strategy is essential to long-term success because it provides benefits through:

1   increasing the ability to be consistent

2   increasing effective diversification

3   removing subjectivity.

Together these benefits not only provide an opportunity to achieve above average rates of return — as proven by some of the world's best investors — but they also help the investor conquer the temptation to rush the process. Quite simply, if a company doesn't meet your criteria — if the share price is too high or too low or if anything does not fit within what we call the acceptable limits of a strategy — you should consider whether it is appropriate.

As the benefit of improving consistency has already been discussed in the previous chapter, only increasing effective diversification and removing subjectivity will be discussed below.

Increasing effective diversification

Diversification means not putting all your eggs in one basket. The way to do this is to spread your risk across and within each asset class. Diversification serves primarily to protect the overall investment return. That is, while one element of the portfolio is doing poorly, some other investment may be doing well and therefore should offset the adverse impact of the poorly performing investment.

The fact remains that for all of the expertise and understanding about the domestic and international economies, we really do not know when or to what extent various sectors of the market will be favourably or adversely performing during a certain period. For this reason, it is important to diversify. By diversifying, the total investment is normally at least partly protected when one element suffers and, perhaps more importantly, the total investment benefits when one element is enjoying favourable economic conditions.

Importantly, proper diversification doesn't simply serve to have the gain on one investment compensate for the loss on the other. Effective diversification should also see the combined total of all investments advance in value as well. Being aware that no investment will do well at all times can help force the investor to adopt a diversified approach. Having an investment strategy can help investors be systematic in their diversification — rather than randomly picking different investments, haing a strategy will ensure they spread their investments across and within asset classes.

It is much easier to diversify within shares than in most other asset classes. Even with smaller amounts of capital it is a simple matter to spread risk across different companies, different industries or different sectors. It is less simple to diversify smaller amounts of capital across different bonds or between commercial, residential and industrial properties.

To determine the behavioural characteristics of Australian share investors, the ASX regularly conducts an Australian share ownership survey. According to the results of the November 2003 survey, 20 per cent of all direct shareholders hold just one share in their portfolio. As a result, their equity investments are hardly diverse.

(Between 2001 and 2003, only 4 per cent of people who invested directly in shares entered the sharemarket for the first time, of which 60 per cent were aged under 35 years. This suggests that it is the younger generation who are more likely to be new entrants into the sharemarket, while the older age group would probably have entered the sharemarket for the first time in the mid- to late nineties with major floats and privatisations.)

This lack of diversity significantly increases the risk associated with their share investments. Any first time investor who enters the market unaware of this fact is particularly vulnerable to market risk.

Risk
Risk is the possibility of misfortune in financial terms, and the uncertainty of future conditions.

Generally speaking, the amount of shares included in a portfolio will be affected initially by the amount available for investment and the costs of investment (including brokerage).

Australian industrial shares usually deliver good real rates of return in the long term. Therefore, it is recommended that investors' portfolios should be structured to achieve significant exposure to this sector, particularly with dividend imputation increasing the after-tax returns to Australian residents.

A diversified approach does not attempt to have small amounts of funds in many different pies — this is ineffective diversification and when transaction costs are included it becomes counterproductive. An improvement is to have larger amounts in a few carefully selected pies. This is diversifying with a strategy.

Dividend imputation
Dividend imputation represents the tax credits passed on to a shareholder who receives a franked dividend. Under provisions of the *Income Tax Assessment Act*, imputation credits entitle investors to a rebate for tax already paid by an Australian company.

Diversify with a strategy — no more than 15 stocks?

Despite its importance, diversification must not become an end in itself. Positive absolute returns are obviously the goal, so it is important that diversification be adopted for the purpose of improving returns. Don't diversify for it's own sake. But how many share investments does it take for your portfolio to be effectively diversified?

Robert Hagstrom in his book *The Warren Buffett portfolio* (John Wiley & Sons 1999) conducted research into the benefits of what is described as 'focus investing'.

The breakdown of portfolios in Hagstrom's study of 12,000 randomly selected portfolios, evenly divided among portfolios with 250, 100, 50 and 15 stocks, looked something like this:

- 3,000 portfolios containing 250 stocks
- 3,000 portfolios containing 100 stocks
- 3,000 portfolios containing 50 stocks
- 3,000 portfolios containing 15 stocks.

The results were surprising. After calculating the average annual return for each portfolio over 10 years and 18 years, Hagstrom discovered the average return for each portfolio was about the same — 13.75 per cent for the 15-stock portfolios rising to 13.91 per cent for the 250-stock portfolios. Startling, however, was the maximum and minimum returns from each of the groups.

Hagstrom's results for the 10-year period of 1987 to 1996 were as as shown in Table 2.1, below.

Table 2.1: Minimum and maximum 10-year returns based on portfolio type

	Minimum RoR	Maximum RoR
15-stock portfolios	4.41%	26.59%
50-stock portfolios	8.62%	19.17%
100-stock portfolios	10.02%	18.32%
250-stock portfolios	11.47%	16.00%

Table 2.2 shows the returns for the 18-year period from 1979 to 1996.

Table 2.2: Minimum and maximum 18-year returns based on portfolio type

	Minimum RoR	Maximum RoR
15-stock portfolios	8.77%	25.04%
50-stock portfolios	13.56%	21.80%
100-stock portfolios	14.71%	20.65%
250-stock portfolios	16.04%	19.20%

From Hagstrom's work it appears obvious that it is the 15-share portfolios that might offer the best possible returns — and, conversely, the worst possible returns. A little further analysis by Hagstrom, however, helped to more accurately define the picture. By comparing returns to the broader market and by examining the question of diversification from a probability perspective, Hagstrom has enabled all investors to reconsider the extent of diversification required.

Here is what he found:

- out of 3,000 15-stock portfolios, 808 beat the market

- out of 3,000 50-stock portfolios, 549 beat the market

- out of 3,000 100-stock portfolios, 337 beat the market

- out of 3,000 250-stock portfolios, 63 beat the market.

Hagstrom submitted the above results as 'convincing evidence' that the probability of beating the market goes up as the number of stocks in a portfolio goes down. There were a higher number of 15-stock portfolios that beat the market and it was these portfolios that offered the best average return and the highest overall return.

Finally, Hagstrom noted that his study did not factor in transaction costs — which, with a 250-stock portfolio, would be significantly higher than a 15-stock portfolio. These higher transaction costs would make it even more difficult for the more broadly diversified portfolios to beat the market.

Transaction costs

Transaction costs (sometimes called 'brokerage') are the costs to have a trade carried out.

Another study which supports the argument for a portfolio of 15 stocks is the study conducted by J. L. Evans and S. H. Archer published in the lauded *Journal of Finance* some years ago. This study revealed that the benefits of diversification accrue as more stocks are added to a portfolio. These benefits, however, cease to accrue at a significant rate after 15 different companies are added to a portfolio. The costs associated with adding a sixteenth company, in fact, are higher than the additional benefit of diversification accrued by the additional company. So, according to Evans and Archer's research, beyond 15 stocks it becomes uneconomical to diversify.

The more stocks you add to a portfolio, the lower the volatility. Eventually, when you own as many stocks as the index, your portfolio looks exactly like the index and so there is no volatility over and above that generated by the index itself. Importantly, however, a portfolio of this type *will not* beat the market. It won't do worse, but it cannot do better.

Correlation — the key to effective diversification

Correlation

Correlation is a statistical measure of the degree to which the movement of two variables is related.

Correlation is the degree to which the movements of two different elements is related. A low correlation means that only a small or minor relationship is observable in the movement of the two elements. A high correlation means that there is a strong relationship between the two. For example, if every time BHP-Billiton moved up in price by $1, RIO also moved up by a similar amount, we could say that BHP-Billiton and RIO are highly positively correlated. They tend to move in the same direction at the same times.

Diversification is effective when investments have low correlation. Be cautious, however, before accepting the idea that low correlation is more important than smart share selection. It is very easy to be carried away with the study of correlation coefficients and build complex portfolios based around the interrelationships between the individual elements of that portfolio. The pursuit of low overall volatility has led, in many cases, to mediocre results. We don't want to purchase a bad investment simply because the share price tends to move down when the others are moving up. If all your investments are moving up, that is a good thing. Furthermore, you must remember that correlation analysis is based on historical price action and there is no guarantee that these relationships will continue. Always apply logic first and then ask if the additional element adds any real value to your existing portfolio.

As you build your portfolio, the portfolio itself becomes a benchmark against which new investments are assessed and determined. The question you may ask is, 'Is this investment better than those I already have?'

The answer to that question takes into account the total portfolio by looking at the new investment's relationship to all the shares already owned, and the individual elements by determining whether this new investment is expected to outperform any existing element. Again, this is diversifying with a strategy.

Figure 2.1, below, shows the result of ineffective diversification. When the market is going well, all investments are rising in value, substantially increasing the value of the portfolio as a whole. When things turn bad the following year, however, all investments fall, compounding the losses of the entire portfolio.

Figure 2.1: Ineffective diversification

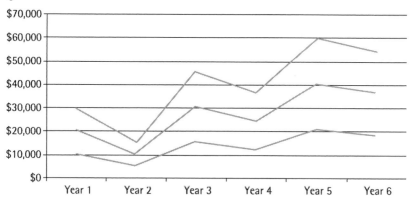

Figure 2.2, overleaf, clearly demonstrates the benefits of the effectively diversified approach. By combining investments that don't move in tandem, the portfolio as a whole enjoys lower volatility in its returns and is certainly preferable on an absolute return basis.

The net result is that, while the portfolio will not do as well as the best performing element of the portfolio, it will do better than the worst performing element. And remember that with the right strategy, over longer periods of time the worst performing element shouldn't be doing too badly anyway.

Figure 2.2: Effective diversification

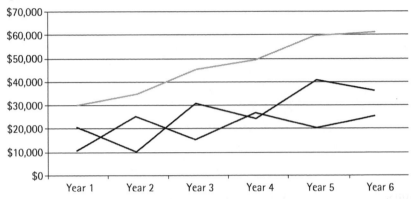

While our discussion about the merits of diversification is not exhaustive, for our purposes it is sufficient to say that implementing a strategy will make it easier to implement an effectively diversified approach.

Removing subjectivity

Many investors form a subjective view of where they think the market or a particular stock will go. That is, they allow their emotions and current circumstances to override any rational analysis.

Consider for a moment whether you think the stock market will go up or down next week on Monday, Tuesday and Wednesday. The answers you could give form eight possible combinations, meaning the probability of you getting them all correct is one-in-eight or 12.5 per cent.

However, when it comes to the markets, less than 12.5 per cent of investors will get it right. Why is that the case? In order for 12.5 per cent of participants to get the direction correct, there has to be an even spread of all eight possible predictions. For example, in a room of 80 people, 10 people will have to select each of the possible choices as shown in Table 2.3, opposite.

Table 2.3: Even spread of predictions

Predictions	Monday	Tuesday	Wednesday
10 x #1:	Down	Down	Up
10 x #2:	Up	Up	Down
10 x #3:	Down	Down	Down
10 x #4:	Up	Up	Up
10 x #5:	Down	Up	Down
10 x #6:	Up	Down	Up
10 x #7:	Up	Down	Down
10 x #8:	Down	Up	Up

The chances of this occurring are very, very slim. Why? The reason is that current market circumstances, news, events and emotions will result in a congregation of selections, rather than an even spread of selections. For example, if the news in the marketplace is bad, a large proportion of investors may tend towards a selection where the majority of the daily movements are down, such as selection one, three, five, or seven.

In the real activity of trading and investing, the investors may position themselves either to take advantage of the expected weakness or avoid it entirely. Their actions once taken, however, remove a large number of participants from the market activity, leaving the market little momentum to continue in that direction. And so it could easily and perversely go in the opposite direction!

Indeed an experienced market participant or a sceptic might conclude that the market will do whatever it must to ensure that the majority who try to pick the daily direction will indeed get it wrong and lose.

Compounding this problem is the fact that the majority of investors either don't have a strategy, fail to stick to their strategy or allow emotions to rule their decision-making. Even fewer will continue to correctly select the direction as more days are added. It becomes obvious when looking at the numbers that the chances of any one person consistently and accurately predicting the direction of the market is extremely slight.

And this is true for the experts as well — even they can get it wrong. While they may defend their stance or point to caveats that were intertwined with the recommendation, it is cold comfort for those investors who bought based on it (although when properly diversified such investments shouldn't pose a hindrance to the growth of the overall portfolio).

Disciplined investors, however, should not be dismayed by these seemingly slim chances of investment success. Once a strategy has been formalised, the process becomes quite straightforward and, coincidentally, quite exciting. The solution is not to give up on the process but to invest with a longer time frame in mind.

We will be looking at strategies in the next chapter to help us select desirable candidates and, ultimately, attempt to beat the market over both the longer term and through short-term speculation.

Now we have emphasised the importance of having a strategy, we can start to formulate a strategy and assess what particular shares we will buy, hold or sell. Chapter 3 looks at the different types of shares available.

Choosing share types and categories

We have already discussed how, by diversifying your share investments (although not too thinly), you can reduce the risk of capital loss and potentially achieve more consistent returns over the longer term. Diversity within shares can be achieved by spreading your investment across individual shares and the various share types and classes available.

This chapter will explore the pros and cons of different share types and categories. There is no one 'right' mix. The best mix for you will be determined by your needs so it is important to use this information to decide which types and categories are going to meet them best. You will also need to consider this when you decide on your asset allocation.

Share types

The types of shares listed and available for trading on the Australian sharemarket are many and varied. Some are looked upon as solid, while others are more speculative. Some are shares in traditional industrial companies and others are in mining start-ups. A further distinction can be made between small-capitalisation companies and those listed on the S&P/ASX 100 or S&P/ASX 200. The first part of this chapter will look at these different 'types' of shares.

Blue chip shares versus speculative shares

Blue chip shares are those of a leading company which is perceived to have good management and a strong financial structure. Those companies generally have a long and consistent history of paying high levels of dividends and other returns to investors, or relatively consistent profit growth. The term 'blue chip' refers to the highest valued gambling chips at casinos and, in the context of investing, it suggests shares with the greatest worth. In practice, however, the actual price of a share does not necessarily determine whether it may be considered a blue chip stock. The term is used to refer to any 'quality' investment.

Dividends
Dividends are an income stream paid to shareholders of some stocks twice yearly by a company out of its profits.

While there is no real disadvantage in owning blue chip shares, not all of them retain that status indefinitely and nor are they guaranteed to provide capital growth or income. Blue chip shares can decrease in price like any other share and their values should be reviewed regularly like all other types of shares.

Speculative shares are those that have not yet established a strong earnings track record and therefore may carry a greater risk that their share price and dividends will remain static or even fall. However, they may have the potential to provide good returns due to, for example, growth in their industry, strong management or gaining market dominance through product development.

Industrial shares versus resource shares

As a share buyer, one of the first questions you will have to answer is whether to choose shares from the industrial sector or the resource sector, or both. These are the two major sectors of the Australian market and the share prices of companies are listed in the Australian media according to which sector they are in.

Industrial companies are those that are in manufacturing or services industries (including financial services). The advantage of industrial shares is that many larger industrial companies tend to declare dividends to their shareholders from their relatively consistent profits. Many companies also pay tax on those profits, making the dividends paid fully or partially franked. This allows their shareholders to receive tax-effective income.

The share price of larger industrial companies can remain relatively stable (that is, the price is less volatile) when compared to some companies in the resource sector. Industrial shares have tended to outperform other asset classes (such as property or bonds) in the long term and they have seldom experienced the short-term volatility that can quickly increase or decrease share prices in the resource sector.

Resource companies include those involved with exploration and the mining of metals and other elements, oil or gas. As at 31 December 2003, they make up approximately 17 per cent of the All Ordinaries.

Initially, many resource companies will explore or mine an area to determine if mineable resources exist. If, for example, oil or gold is discovered, shares in the company will quickly come into demand, usually raising the share price dramatically. This gives the investor the potential to benefit from dramatic growth in a short period of time.

However, the obvious disadvantage in some resource shares is that exploration could continue indefinitely without solid results. The company may have to eventually give up the search to move to another area or even wind down. Mines are also a wasting asset because, as the minerals are dug out of the ground, the value of the discovery must diminish over time.

The directors of resource companies generally keep a larger slice of the profits for reinvestment into the company, so many mining companies pay little or no dividends to the investor. Instead, the reinvestment helps to expand the company with the aim of increased share price growth in the future.

The Australian resources market is more difficult to value than the industrials, as earnings from this particular sector have been much more volatile in the past. Metal prices and exchange rates fluctuate daily, and a small change in the Australian dollar selling price can have a much greater

Franking

Franking is the process of paying dividends out of after-tax profits.

For more information on franked dividends and taxation, see Chapter 18.

impact on the earnings per share of a resources sector company — the main earnings of which come from exports — than an industrial company.

Some companies listed on ASX, however, are involved in both the industrial and mining sectors — the most obvious example being BHP Billiton.

Small capitalisation shares versus S&P/ASX indices

Large financial institutions, such as superannuation funds and insurance companies, oversee the investment and security of billions of dollars of investment funds. These indirect investments belong to Australian workers and insurance holders and should be kept safely in trust by the institutions in charge of the funds. Nearly all of those institutions invest a considerable portion of the funds in shares, so their fund managers are in constant touch with sharemarket analysts and experts who recommend stocks that they expect will perform well in the future. Almost without exception, their recommendations reflect the preference of most fund managers for investing in large companies offering low volatility, strong performance and high liquidity, rather than smaller companies with low liquidity or turnover, or a limited record of business success.

This preference for larger companies with higher liquidity means that those companies included in the main S&P/ASX indices, especially the top 50 or 100 shares, are generally more regularly traded by institutions. Remember — institutions can be in charge of millions of dollars, so their decision to buy or sell any particular share can significantly affect its share price.

The fact that the majority of fund managers concentrate on shares in the S&P/ASX 100 and S&P/ASX 200 underlines their importance as indicators of the Australian sharemarket's performance. Approximately 97 per cent of all sharemarket turnover comes from those companies included in the ASX All Ordinaries, which represents the top 500 companies.

Indirect investments
Indirect investments are those made by a fund or trust in a range of assets or securities on your behalf.

Liquidity
Liquidity is the ease with which an asset can be converted to cash without suffering a loss in value.

All Ordinaries
The All Ordinaries or All Ords is a measure of the overall performance of the Australian sharemarket at any given point in time. It is made up of the share prices for 500 of the largest Australian companies.

The funds' concentration on the companies that make up the All Ordinaries tends to reduce the funds available for investment in the smaller capitalised shares. This means that individual investors may be able to take advantage of investment opportunities that arise in small-capitalisation companies — for example, if the share price is trading at lower than the investor's analysis of its worth. Further, when a smaller capitalised company excels, its share price may rise significantly, providing profit opportunities and increasing its market capitalisation to the point that it too is included in the All Ords. This will cause its shares to be purchased by the large institutional funds, further increasing the company's liquidity.

One disadvantage for small-capitalisation companies is that some sharemarket experts suggest that larger companies, which require larger amounts of capital for their specific projects, can borrow at lower interest rates than smaller companies and may even be able to compete better internationally. The shares of these largest companies are often more acceptable to institutions and overseas investors, with some companies even quoting their shares on other international share exchanges. For example, BHP-Billiton has its shares listed in London and Australia.

A second disadvantage for smaller capitalised companies is that, while some firms analyse selected small companies, many stockbroking firms employ research staff primarily to analyse the larger companies. While this increases the potential for individual investors to spot an opportunity the big firms have missed, it diminishes the number of research reports on smaller companies that might otherwise be distributed to stockbrokers' clients. Some medium-sized listed companies rely on niche stockbrokers to analyse the company and recommend its shares to investors, while those companies among the bottom (300 to 400) companies of the All Ords may have very few stockbroking firms analysing them at all. Because few investors can access detailed research about the smaller companies, they are less able to analyse whether they represent an investment opportunity and may perceive them

Market capitalisation
Market capitalisation is the market value of a company. It is calculated by multiplying the number of ordinary shares on issue by the current share price.

to be less attractive than those they know much more about. This can result in lower levels of liquidity for the smaller companies.

The Australian Stock Exchange, however, compiles data on every company listed, and makes a selection of products such as company profiles and share price histories available to the stockbroking community, share investors and the general public through ASX customer service (1300 300 279) or via email (info@asx.com.au).

Share categories

Most of the time when we talk about 'shares' or 'equities' we mean ordinary shares. The majority of shares traded in Australia are ordinary shares but other share categories do exist so we will offer an explanation of these in this section.

Ordinary shares

Ordinary shares typically represent the bulk of a company's ownership capital. As this class of share carries the voting rights, the owners of ordinary shares effectively control the company. Many companies, however, issue tens of thousands of shares and most private investors owning a thousand or so shares will have little effect on how a company is run. Institutional investors and some lobby groups have in the past got together to influence how a company has been run. Ordinary shareholders will also receive any dividends paid.

For more information on ordinary shares, see *Starting out in shares – the ASX way.*

Preference shares

Preference shares entitle the shareholder to preferred dividend payments at a fixed rate over ordinary shares. They also have priority over ordinary shareholders for repayment of capital in the event of the company being wound up. Companies can issue a variety of preference shares, such as convertible, cumulative, participating or redeemable, and many have an individual combination of characteristics, rights and privileges — for example, limited voting rights.

One of the most popular forms of preference shares is the convertible security. Convertible securities are hybrids, having features of both fixed-interest investments and shares. They pay an income to the investor, who later has a choice of converting the security into ordinary shares or redeeming it for cash. This limits the potential loss an investor can incur. For example, if things go well, it might be beneficial to convert the security into shares, as its value is likely to move in line with that of the company's shares. But if things are not going well, the security can be redeemed for its face value.

There are several different types of convertible securities. Some can be converted to ordinary shares by a specified date, either automatically (in that they have to be converted on that date) or at the request of the holder prior to that date. This type of convertible preference share usually gives a fixed rate of dividend, often higher than that given to the ordinary shareholder. They can also participate in rights and bonus issues as if they had already been converted. When the market price of the company's ordinary share increases, the value of the convertible security goes up, usually to the same extent.

Other types include converting preference shares that are compulsorily convertible to ordinary shares, usually at a discount to the market price of the company's share on the conversion date. However, with converting preference shares, a change in the price of the company's shares will not change the market price of the preference shares as the security conversion process involves calculations with dollars, not shares.

Convertible unsecured notes, better known as convertible notes, are used to convert a loan to the company into ordinary shares at a specific ratio. Until converted, these notes are the same as a loan security in that they give priority to the noteholder over normal shareholders in the event of liquidation of the company. They also usually give interest income higher than the normal income received from dividends. However, interest income from the convertible notes, like any interest income, is fully taxable. The interest income cannot be franked — unlike the dividends from convertible preference shares, which may or may not be franked depending on the company.

Another feature of these types of securities is that they give the convertible security holder the other benefits given to ordinary shareholders — for example, shareholder discounts. On the downside, although convertible securities may give a set guaranteed interest or yield, they often exist at a premium to the ordinary share price, causing the investor to sustain a capital loss when they are converted.

Nonetheless, some investors are prepared to accept this loss in exchange for the income.

As well as identifying the shares most suitable for your portfolio, you will need to know how to decide what you think is a 'fair value' for a particular security. To do this, you will have to consider the price to net tangible assets ratio per share, the price/earnings ratio, the gross dividend yield (including imputation credits), the likely growth in future earnings per share and the ratio of the earnings before interest, depreciation and tax to the total liabilities of the company. But we're getting ahead of ourselves — the different ways to approach stock selection are covered in the next few chapters.

4 Getting started

There are many stock selection methods used in the attempt to generate and accumulate long-term wealth through the sharemarket. We cannot possibly hope to cover every method available but throughout the next few chapters we will examine a few of the ways that have curiously robust historical track records. In these chapters, the following stock selection methods will be covered in some detail:

- value investing
- growth investing
- growth at a reasonable price (GARP) investing
- investing for income
- ethical investing
- market neutral investing.

We will also examine the styles of the expert money managers.

Of course, we would not prescribe which, if any, of these methods you should use. As already discussed, you must develop a method or strategy that suits you and stick with it during adverse periods. Take the information on different strategies provided over the following chapters and develop something you are comfortable with. To help you

Fundamental analysis

Fundamental analysis is the analysis of a security or issuer, taking into account such factors as past and forecast performance figures, the nature of the business, market position, management and general economic factors.

do that, this chapter will discuss what you need to do to get started in buying and selling shares. This discussion is followed in Chapter 5 by a descriptive overview of the more important ratios that are used in fundamental analysis, since the technique of fundamental analysis is common to all the stock selection methods and strategies discussed in the following chapters.

First, let's look at the steps involved in getting started as an investor who is looking to trade shares on a more regular basis. The steps are:

- gather information
- choose a universe of potential investments to investigate
- find the tools to help make your investment decisions.

Gather information

Let's explore the various sources of information that are available to garner the data necessary to make informed share trading decisions and consider the merits of each stock.

Historical fundamental data

Fundamental data is the information that is provided by a company about its financial position and performance through the balance sheet, the profit and loss statement and the cash flow statement. By definition, it is historical. For active long-term investors, it is imperative that a sound understanding of the fundamentals of a company is obtained as this allows investment decisions to become more logical and rational, and less emotional.

Historical fundamental analysis can help investors determine the quality of a business. Quality is a critical issue that relates not only to the business itself, its market dominance or its growth potential, but also to its people, particularly its management. For some businesses, determining the quality of the business and its management can be difficult, particularly if the investor is not able to speak to management or look at historical information. New businesses in emerging industries are particularly hard to assess, as there are a multitude of variables and determining influences conspiring to thwart the efforts of the sharebuyer in determining quality and assessing risks.

For older businesses with a long history, assessing quality becomes substantially easier but by no means simple. A track record does, however, give the sharebuyer a measuring rod with which to assess risk and compare options.

There are a number of sources of historical fundamental data available in both hard copy format and electronically through web-based subscriber services and analysis software.

Stockbrokers' reviews and recommendations

Some brokers will provide annual and semi-annual reviews of all the companies covered by their own research departments. While the reviews and recommendations may later prove valuable, for now we are only interested in the historical fundamental data for each company.

Earnings estimates and price forecasts

More advanced traders may add experts' earnings estimates and forecasts to their stable of analysis tools. By examining what the experts think the future holds for a specific company, a more useful appraisal can be determined. We say more useful because 'market events cast their shadow before them'. That is, future share prices will be determined by how the company performs in the future, not how it has performed in the past.

As forecasting requires some expertise and certainly some knowledge of the industry, the best source of this information is usually the research departments of stockbroking firms. In many instances, the analysts employed by the broking firms have the benefit of meeting with company management to discuss the outlook for the company and the industry. This research can then be combined with in-house economic analysis to assess the likely impact of economic growth, interest rates, inflation and government policy on the outlook for the company.

The impact of interest rates and inflation on companies is discussed in greater detail in Chapter 12.

A word of warning, however — when you are considering what shares to trade you should always question forecasts if they are being used as part of the stock selection process. Forecasts have a consistent habit of being changed as circumstances evolve and, importantly, companies often either beat or fail to meet the forecasts attributed to their earnings.

Charts

We will examine some charts as part of our technical analysis discussion in Chapter 12. It is enough to remember here that charts are a source of information and therefore may contribute to the stock selection decision-making process. There is definitely some merit in the use of charts or technical analysis, and the source of such charts are many and varied. While some are relatively inexpensive, they may not be comprehensive enough to fulfil all the needs of share traders as they develop their skills. Others can cost more than $7,000 — and can go even as high as $10,000. However, such sums might be better invested rather than spent on tools that may be significantly more comprehensive than will ever be required.

Technical analysis

Technical analysis is the analysis of a security which looks at the technicals — that is, the charting patterns and technical indicators made up from movements in the share price — to form an option of the historical and future price trends.

News

The news media is an essential source of information. It provides a second and third opinion and in doing so may even offer another perspective for the investor. The danger, however, is for investors who don't have their own disciplined investing strategy. This is because news is written by people and these people, like all others, are emotional creatures. As such, stories may contain a healthy dollop of emotion, meaning subjectivity becomes a serious issue. For this reason, relying on the news as a sole source of information can be dangerous and is often the reason some investors feel as though they are constantly chasing their tails.

Company announcements

These are the words on which the daily fluctuations of the market hang. Companies provide a steady 'speculating account' of information to the market, allowing the investor to make informed assessments about the suitability of a particular company's shares for their portfolio. The speed with which the market reacts to these announcements, however, does not usually provide the opportunity for private investors to make speculative plays.

The company announcements are, nevertheless, important to the active investor. Those providing information about the prospects of a company's outlook and those describing growth strategies by senior company board members or the CEO are of particular use.

The Australian Stock Exchange's continuous disclosure regime is based on the principle that information which may affect security values or influence investment decisions must be disclosed.

In general, listed companies must lodge the following with ASX:

- annual report
- half yearly report
- preliminary final report
- half yearly ASIC accounts
- annual audited financial statements lodged with ASIC
- quarterly cash flow report — only required for mining exploration entities and commitments test entities
- quarterly activities report —for mining exploration or production entities
- takeover information
- security holder notifications.

Choose a universe

The next step is an important one. A share trader cannot begin to expect to track and follow every company and every security in the marketplace. There are simply too many. While the 'stock market' is the ultimate universe from which candidates will be selected, it is important to be mindful that finding those candidates is the end result of a process that involves narrowing the field to the 'more likely' candidates.

It's no surprise that major broking firms, banks and research outfits employ analysts who specialise in one or two particular fields, sectors or industries. This is because we cannot become sufficiently expert in everything. For this reason alone it is necessary to narrow the field of possible options to a smaller group. This group is referred to as our universe.

You can speculate outside of the universe if opportunities arise or are offered; however, for the investing or long-term account, have a set number of securities to watch.

We have already made the point that Warren Buffett didn't invest in technology stocks during the tech boom of the late 1990s, but perhaps less well known is the reason why. Interestingly, it was not because he thought there were no opportunities in the sector or that the sector has not merit. He didn't invest in technology because technology did not fall into his sphere of understanding. There is a great deal of merit in the adage, 'Stick to what you know'.

Find the tools to help make your investment decisions

The decision to invest in a particular company can be made a number of ways. The investor may elect to purchase a stock based purely on the fundamental merits of that company after looking at its profits and/or profitability, and its assets and liabilities, or after comparing the price to various aspects of the company's profit and loss statement, balance sheet or cash flow statement. Alternatively, the investor could use the price action of the stock itself shown on charts to trigger a trade. Or he or she could use a combination of the two.

Some of the techniques available include:

- fundamental analysis

- classic technical analysis

- quantitative analysis (mechanical).

Technical and mechanical analysis will be looked at in Chapter 12. However, for the skills required for long-term investment, we will look at fundamental analysis.

5 Fundamental analysis

Fundamental analysis is the study of the various factors that affect a company's earnings and dividends as well as the impact on the relative safety of an investment in a certain company due to the relationship between its share price and the various elements of its financial position and performance.

Fundamental analysis also involves a detailed examination of the company's competitors, the industry or sector it is within, and perhaps even the entire domestic and global economic climate. Fundamental analysts may examine the growth prospects for the sector. Future levels of general economic activity are also used to help determine whether a company's prospects are improving or not.

Fundamental analysis can be quantitative, which involves looking at the hard numbers and either developing benchmarks or hurdles for the individual company to exceed or ranking companies by the resultant ratios. Fundamental analysis can also be qualitative. Qualitative analysis is more subjective — for example, it may be a discussion with the directors of the company about their growth prospects or it could be a chat in the street with a customer, an employee or even a competitor's staff member.

Fund managers may meet with the board of directors of a company, or even be on the board.

Fundamental analysis is forward looking even though the data used is by and large historical. This raises an important limitation of fundamental analysis, as we will see.

Factors that may be analysed through fundamental analysis include:

- the quality of the management team
- the background of the directors
- the current, past and projected earnings
- the industry the company is a part of
- demand prospects for the company's goods and/or services
- the relative competitive advantage of the company
- debt levels and interest rates
- ratio analysis of the company
- announcements subject to ASX listing rules.

Intrinsic value
Intrinsic value is the actual value or book price of a security, as opposed to its current market value. The measurement of intrinsic value is subjective and dependent on the valuation method used.

The objective of fundamental analysis is to determine what the company should be worth or its 'intrinsic value', and/or its growth prospects. This intrinsic value can then be compared to the current value of the company as measured by the share price and market capitalisation. If the shares are trading at less than the intrinsic value, the shares may be seen as good value or as offering a relative cheap 'entry' price. If, however, the intrinsic value calculated by the fundamental analyst is lower than the current share price, the analysts may place a sell recommendation on the shares or, at best, a hold recommendation.

It is essential to gain a sound understanding of how to value shares and measure the efficiency and profitability of a business and its management.

One aspect of fundamental analysis that we will be examining more closely is ratio analysis and the importance of some of the many ratios. We will also look at the limitation of this analysis — not to diminish the possible worth of the tools but because a sound understanding of the limits will ensure caution is still applied to the investing process. As Charlie Munger — Warren Buffett's partner at Berkshire Hathaway — said, 'To a man with a hammer, every problem looks like a nail'. When arming a person with a hammer, it makes sense to also show what the hammer can and cannot do.

Even with a simple summary of the main sources of company information, it becomes easy to see why private investors and traders shy away from conducting their own analysis. Seeing it as mumbo jumbo, accounting speak, chasing a moving beast and/or looking at the past, there are plenty of people who would rather do something else. And many people do. The rise in popularity of charting, astrology, waves and cycles is, in part, evidence of investors' rejection of anything that seems difficult or boring. Much of the work in fundamental analysis, however, has already been done for you and there is often little need to re-invent the wheel.

Even if you don't become a master of analysis, you will benefit from a working knowledge of financial statements and press reports. Being able to interpret the data at least provides a crosscheck to the conclusions drawn from other approaches.

What are you trying to learn about the company?

Share investors must be clear about what knowledge they are seeking. There are some basic principles that should be remembered and questions that should be asked. While not exhaustive, the following list provides a helpful starting point:

- Check where the projected growth is going to come from.

- Don't draw conclusions from a single financial item in isolation.

- Companies are multidimensional. For example, debt funding might have increased dramatically. While this may initially be perceived as a negative if there are no sales to help generate cash to pay the interest, it could be a positive if used correctly. Indeed, not enough debt can also be viewed as suboptimal.

- Historical costs give a poor approximation to real values.

- Consolidated statements could be hiding poor results in a particular sector of the group.

- The financial profile of a company should, at worst, reflect the industry it belongs to and, at best, stand out as the benchmark for that industry. An important question therefore is, 'What is the typical structure for the industry?'

Detailed questions to ask include:

- Is turnover keeping pace with the sector and with the competitors?

- Is the growth in turnover being achieved organically or through acquisition? (If acquired, will turnover remain the same once fully integrated into the company?)

- Is the profit margin growing? Is it too high compared to competitors? If it is very high, new competitors will enter on price reducing margins. On the other hand, a low margin could suggest control of the cost base has been lost or factors outside the company's control are squeezing margins.

- To what extent do current profits reflect one-off events?

- Will the profits and growth rates be sustainable over the longer term? This depends on industry structural issues (how many competitors) as well as the economy. What is the company's pricing power? Are there natural barriers to entry that may prevent a competitor from entering and reducing prices?

Relating to the last question on the above list, PC manufacturers are an excellent example of how competition reduces prices. Are PC prices rising or falling? Clearly, they are falling. Attempting to work out revenues and profits in this sector for the next decade or so is extremely difficult and under these circumstances, individual investors and many professional analysts are simply speculating when they attempt to determine a value for these businesses.

In fundamental analysis, in-depth research into a company is compiled. Several statements are examined. These include the company's:

- balance sheet

- profit and loss statement

- cash flow statement

- letter to shareholders.

Before undertaking the task of examining some of the important ratios used in fundamental analysis, a few points are worth noting. Firstly, we are not preparing you to become qualified analysts or licensed advisers — and even being qualified or licensed does not immediately confer upon you the status of 'successful share trader'. Secondly, not every ratio will be covered — for the same reason. Finally, and perhaps most importantly, we do not open the ratios up to interpretation in this book. It is appropriate in an introductory text to tie the description of the ratios in with an interpretation of that ratio.

See *Starting out in shares — the ASX way* for an introduction to ratios and how to interpret them.

Market ratios

A basic step towards successful investing is to relate a company's performance to the price of its shares. By calculating 'per share' data we can compare earnings, corporate health and even debt to a company's share price.

However, any ratios that are based on the market price of a share need to be used with caution as there are many factors (several of them not controllable or measurable) that affect the traded price of a share. Here is a list of some of the factors that may influence a share price and yet have very little to do with the company's fundamental position or performance:

- expectations of future flow of dividends
- level of perceived risk related to the nature of the business
- the possibility or hope of a takeover
- fluctuations in interest rates
- weekly or even daily speculation about a company's earnings
- overseas market sentiment
- politics
- wars
- fear, greed, hope and panic.

The way supply and demand, and earnings affect share prices is discussed below, prior to our analysis of market ratios.

Supply and demand affect share prices

All things being equal, if the supply of a good were to increase, its price should fall. Similarly, if its supply were to fall, its price would rise. These simple economic laws remain true in the stock market. If the supply of a stock were to increase through a placement, a bonus issue or a rights issue, all things being equal its price should fall. One of the simple rules of thumb is that investors should avoid companies that have a long-term history of constantly issuing new stock. If, for example, a company were to reduce the supply of its shares, the share price should rise. This is why news of a buy-back by a company of its shares is usually seen as a positive development.

Even more simply, suppose a company's shares were trading at $1 and it was expected the company would announce a 10 cent dividend. The company, however, announces a 20 cent dividend due to a better than expected profit which in turn was due to cost cutting and growth in revenue. You would expect demand for the company's shares to be higher. This higher demand translates to buying and this buying pushes the price higher. The news may also reduce supply as existing shareholders decide they don't want to sell their shares. Either way the price rises.

From time to time companies announce capital raisings that will increase the number of shareholders, and yet the prices for the underlying shares rise. A curious development you might say, and one based mostly on the hope that the funds will be used productively to take advantage of cheaper acquisition prices. Provided these expectations are met, the shares may remain elevated. However, if the company should fail to deliver, the larger number of shares means that the profits must necessarily be spread around more thinly than previously.

Earnings affect share prices

In his model for reflexivity, one of the world's most infamous speculators, George Soros, explains that one of the main drivers of share prices is a company's earnings. As earnings rise and are retained by the company, the value of the shares to the shareholder rises and so the price of the shares also rises as investors, keen to gain access to the higher earnings, become increasingly willing to pay the higher prices.

Soros's model is shown in Figure 5.1, overleaf. In the model, it is evident that as the earnings rise, the share price also rises. Just as the share price starts to rise, however, you will notice some divergence. See how the share price is falling even though the earnings are still rising? What is happening here? Has the market got it wrong? On the contrary — the market is looking ahead. The market believes the high share price has factored-in or taken into account the very best the company could produce and the market is now looking ahead. The market perhaps expects future declines in earnings and sell offs in anticipation of this future decline. Investors who have held the stock for some time perhaps believe this is all they are going to get and taking profits becomes an important objective.

However, when earnings continue to rise, more buyers enter the market and more favourable reports are published in the media. This enthusiasm pushes the share price above earnings per share. With time, however, the over-optimistic bias is recognised as such and expectations lower, causing prices to plummet to a point below earnings. The underlying earnings trend reverses, which reinforces the drop in prices. Finally, the pessimism of the market stabilises and the cycle moves back to its starting point.

Figure 5.1: Soros model of reflexivity

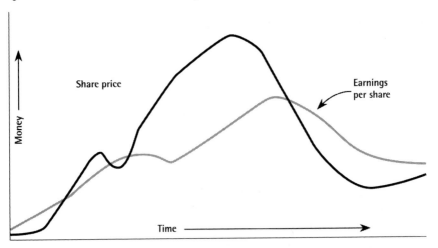

From: *Alchemy of finance* by George Soros, p. 53 Copyright (c) 1994 by George Soros. Reprinted with permission of John Wiley & Sons, Inc.

With that understanding of how supply, demand and expectations regarding earnings affect share prices, we will now look at a number of important market ratios.

Earnings per share (EPS)

The earnings per share of a company is found using the formula below.

$$\text{EPS} = \frac{\text{net profit after tax (NPAT)}}{\text{number of shares on issue}} = \text{cents per share}$$

An EPS figure on its own means very little. It could include non-recurring items, so it is important that the analyst looks at net profit after tax but before any of these non-recurring items referred to as 'abnormal items'. Further, the company may not necessarily pay this amount out as a dividend.

For the successful share investor, it is important to check whether the EPS has been rising or at least has been relatively stable. While this requirement will be dependent on the strategy selected, the criterion of a stable or rising earnings stream over many years could certainly prevent investment in companies that are later liquidated and delisted at a loss to the investor.

From the formula, it is easy to see that there are only two ways EPS can fall — either profits decline or the number of shares increases. For the active investor, generally speaking, too much of either is not a good thing. A lower profit means the investor earns less and a larger number of shareholders to share the profit with also means less profits.

After determining the current EPS, look for trends. Has EPS been growing or falling, and how much profit is from operations rather than once-off events? If EPS is the same as last year, has there been an increase in the shares on issue? Remember — EPS doesn't lend itself to the determination of 'quality'. In bear markets, analysts look much more closely at the quality earnings and quickly dismiss one-off items in an attempt to appear more conservative. During good times, however, even some individual brokers may be pressuring analysts to be a little more relaxed and less conservative.

Price/earnings ratio

The price/earnings ratio (P/E ratio) shows how many times, in years, it will take for your purchase to be covered by earnings. It is determined by using the formula below.

$$\text{P/E ratio} = \frac{\text{share price}}{\text{EPS}} = \text{times covered by earnings}$$

This is one of the easiest to use ratios. The P/E ratio provides an immediate comparison tool. Investors must realise, however, that P/E ratios are often based on historical earnings and therefore may be of little real use in determining a share's value. It may be more important and more useful to use prospective earnings in the P/E ratio calculation.

The P/E ratio reflects the market's view of the earnings potential of the company.

A low P/E ratio compared to the average P/E of the sector that the company belongs to could indicate three things, either:

- the stock is underpriced

- the stock is correctly priced due to the quality (or lack thereof) of the earnings

- the shares are overpriced because the entire sector has become fashionable and the earnings are unsustainable.

Time and again, high P/Es have been shown to be based more on faith (or hype) than on substance, but solidly performing growth-oriented companies tend to have consistently higher P/E ratios. On its own, however, the P/E ratio really doesn't say very much. It is much more effective when used in conjunction with other measures, such as return on equity, discussed later in this chapter.

Dividend per share (DPS)

Dividend per share is simply the earnings payout received in your hand in cents per share, as shown below.

$$\text{DPS} \quad = \quad \frac{\text{total dividend paid}}{\text{number of shares on issue}} \quad = \quad \text{cents per share}$$

A thorough analyst does not merely observe consistent dividend payment over many years and then determine the investment to be 'safe' or the company a 'blue chip'. It is essential to check if the dividends were paid from the current year's earnings or from retained earnings of previous years.

To do that, you can check the payout ratio or dividends/earnings, which shows what percentage of earnings was paid out as a dividend. The reciprocal is earnings/dividends, which is the dividend cover ratio. If the dividend cover ratio is less than one, the dividends must have been paid out of retained earnings.

Dividend cover ratio
The dividend cover ratio is how many times current earnings cover the dividend paid.

Sometimes paying out all the earnings as dividends is not a good thing — for example, perhaps an above average rate of return could be gained from using the money to fund expansion or an acquisition instead of paying dividends. At other times, if the company can't do anything with the earnings, it will pay out a special dividend or announce a return of capital. For shareholders in good quality companies, it may be an advantage for the company and the remaining shareholders if funds were used in a share buyback.

Dividend yield

The dividend yield is the dividend expressed as a percentage of the share price, as shown in the formula below.

$$\text{Dividend yield} = \frac{\text{dividends per share}}{\text{share price}} \times 100 = \%$$

This is the rate that can be used to compare the income generated from one investment to that from another. Later we'll see that, due to the benefits of franking, a dividend yield of 5 per cent can be more beneficial than earning interest of 5 per cent.

High dividend yields are attractive but even if a company is showing a dividend yield of 11 per cent and every other company in the same sector is showing dividend yields of 5 per cent, it may not mean that the company under investigation is going to pay a high dividend. The above formula for determining the dividend yield shows there are two components that determine the yield — last year's dividend and the price. A high dividend yield may have been driven by a lower share price and, given that the dividend yield is based on last year's dividend, the lower price may indicate that the market expects next year's dividend to be lower. Nevertheless, as we will see later, market participants regularly panic, driving prices down in expectation of significantly lower dividends, only to find later that their pessimism was unfounded. The dividend yield can therefore be used to highlight companies that are unduly oppressed by market pessimism. These factors, and their caveats, will be explained later once we start building some strategies.

Cash flow per share

The formula for cash flow per share is shown below.

$$\text{Cash flow per share} = \frac{\text{NPAT} + \text{depreciation}}{\text{number of shares on issue}} = \text{cents per share}$$

In the formula to determine cash flow per share, you will note that most analysts add back depreciation because it is a non-cash expense. By adding back the depreciation (and other non-cash expenses), we arrive at a proxy for the cash earnings of the business.

Cash is an extremely important part of evaluating a company and it becomes even more important when the economy slows and company earnings are being examined with more scrutiny. The 'cash is king' adage is rarely considered during periods of boom when momentum investing and growth strategies take the fore. The first hint of slowing growth or the first mention of the word 'recession' and professionals in the market begin touting the benefits of defensive strategies.

'Defensive' can mean a number of things — it can mean finding companies with earnings that are shielded from the slowing economy or are derived predominantly from a country that is not subject to the slowdown. It can also mean finding companies with either a large proportion of their earnings in cash or large cash reserves. Companies with large amounts of cash or cash earnings are considered good options with defensive strategies because they are able to weather the storm and continue to pay out cash dividends or pay down some of their debt. For these reasons, focusing on cash may be a worthwhile endeavour.

Capital ratios

Capital ratios measure management's efficiency in the use of a company's capital and are an important indicator of a company's long-term stability. The most important capital ratios for our purposes are the debt to equity ratios which indicate the company's level of gearing. The formulas for these ratios are below.

$$\text{Debt to equity ratio} = \frac{\text{total borrowings}}{\text{shareholders' equity}} \times 100 = \%$$

$$\text{Net debt to equity ratio} = \frac{\text{total borrowings} - \text{cash}}{\text{shareholders' equity}} \times 100 = \%$$

There are principally two sources of funding for a company — debt and equity. The question for the company is what is the right mix. A company with a high proportion of debt is said to be highly leveraged or geared. Should the entity borrow more money or raise capital through the issue of shares? Doctorates have been devoted, and chairs endowed, to the pursuit of finding the right mix. Measures such as the weighted average cost of capital have been devised and many academics and investors swear by this and the various models that have been developed to determine the correct mix and which source of funding to use for a given project.

To many, the analysis of such decision making may seem essential. However, success in the game of investing is not devoted to the most intelligent. As Warren Buffett once quipped, 'Investing is not a game where the guy with the 160 IQ beats the guy with the 130 IQ'.[1]

Generally, debt is regarded as a cheaper source of funds than equity and so the higher the debt levels the better the return on the equity. Too high a debt level and the margin

---

1   Source: Robert G. Hagstrom, *The Warren Buffett portfolio*, John Wiley & Sons, 1999.

of safety for a company begins to erode so while it is important that debt is used, the company should not overextend itself. Nevertheless, if equity levels are too high compared to debt, the return to shareholders will be lower.

There are other disadvantages of too much debt. Credit ratings can be compromised and the cost of funding the debt can rise if interest rates increase. During times of low interest rates, this is often not a concern; however, if interest rates rise, the cost of funding the debt could become onerous. For these reasons it is important that management must strike an appropriate balance.

To assess the correct level we need to ask 'what-if' questions — for example, how would cash flows be affected if a recession were to transpire or if interest rates went up?

Profitability ratios

Profitability ratios are the basic test of a company's profit performance. Three important profitability ratios are return on equity, return on assets and profit margin, as shown below.

$$\text{Return on equity} = \frac{\text{NPAT}}{\text{shareholders' equity}} \times 100 = \%$$

$$\text{Return on assets} = \frac{\text{earnings before interest and tax (EBIT)}}{\text{total assets}} \times 100 = \%$$

$$\text{Profit margin} = \frac{\text{NPAT}}{\text{sales revenue}} \times 100 = \%$$

Profitability ratios measure a company's ability to earn solid, high, sustainable and/or non-volatile profits. They measure the return the company is making on funds or other resources it has at its disposal. The return generated here, however, is not the same as that which the shareholders receive, as not all the earnings generated are paid out as dividends. Indeed, sometimes no dividends are paid out at all and the profits are reinvested by the company.

The numbers generated by these profitability ratios reflect how clever the company has been in earning money on the funds invested by the shareholders. The ability of a company to earn a decent return means it can attract future funding, perhaps at more desirable rates, and management may also gain favour with the investment community.

The results are generally an indication of a company's financial wellbeing. The greater the amount of money that a company can generate, the more it can grow, and, as we mentioned earlier, it is growth that is necessary for long-term sustained price increases.

Importantly, the investor should remember that profitability is different from absolute profits. Profitability is the rate of return over some other part of the business — such as what the investors have entrusted to management (equity), the total resources at management's disposal (assets), or the sales that the company generates.

As a shareholder, you are an owner and as such it is you who takes on the risk of whether a company can earn a sustainable profit over a number of years. The value of the shares you hold depends firstly on the profit-making record of the entity. So these numbers produce some of the most important indications of the quality of the business you own or are considering owning a part of.

Also worth mentioning is that it is through these ratios that most of the adjustments are made and numbers tinkered with by analysts. For example:

- Extraordinary and/or abnormal items can be taken out to better reflect true recurring after-tax profits, meaning the figure used is often net profit after tax but before abnormal items.

- Share issues and various classes of shares (such as bonus issues and rights issues, and company options) are adjusted for to more accurately reflect the return to ordinary shareholders. The profit figures given after these adjustments are called 'fully diluted earnings'.

Liquidity ratios

Liquidity ratios show a company's ability to pay its short-term debt and the amount that shareholders would receive should the company be liquidated. Three important liquidity ratios are the current ratio, the quick ratio and net tangible asset (NTA) backing. The formulas for these are shown below.

$$\text{Current ratio} = \frac{\text{current assets}}{\text{current liabilities}} = \text{times covered}$$

$$\text{Quick ratio} = \frac{\text{current assets} - \text{inventories}}{\text{current liabilities}} = \text{times covered}$$

$$\text{NTA backing} = \frac{\text{shareholders' equity} - \text{intangibles}}{\text{number of shares on issue}} = \text{cents per share}$$

Appropriate numbers for the liquidity ratios are crucial to the survival of a business, particularly during times of adversity. If short-term assets are less than short-term liabilities, the company may be insolvent and, under corporations law, operating while insolvent is an offence. Failure to pay down debts on time can also hurt a company's credit ratings and future cost of funds, and even threaten its existence.

The current ratio is also known as the working capital ratio. It measures the excess of current assets over current liabilities and so, in turn, it measures short-term liquidity of the company and its ability to meet short-term debt obligations.

The general rule of thumb for a current ratio is 2 to 1 — that is, $2 of current assets for every $1 of current liabilities. Importantly, this general rule will not change regardless of the strategy employed.

Each industry's activity cycle, however, will be a different length. The activity cycle is the time that elapses between money being paid out for the purchase of raw material or goods and the revenue being received upon sale of the company's products. Longer activity cycles suggest a company will take longer to be paid and this must be supported by a higher current ratio.

There are plenty of hurdles prior to the revenue generation stage and receipt of funds. Processing of raw materials, construction, drying, shipping, importing and exporting are all steps in the activity cycle for various industries. If interest is owed in the short term, cash flow must be carefully managed and a buffer of current assets, particularly cash and its equivalents, must be available to meet payments as and when they fall due.

The quick ratio, or acid test ratio, is similar to the current ratio described above; however, the quick ratio removes inventory and looks at what assets can contribute to cash in the next month or two to help meet liabilities due for payment during that period. With the quick ratio we can assess what the implications for short-term debt facilitation might be if a company suffered slowing inventory sales.

Net tangible assets, or NTA, backing of a share describes what each share is worth if all assets were sold (in an orderly manner) and all debts paid and the residual was paid out to shareholders on a per share basis. In a forced liquidation, however — and it usually is forced as there are few reasons to wind up a well-run and profitable business — assets rarely realise their book value. They are being sold during times of pressure on asset prices due to poor economic conditions. The NTA backing figure also suffers from the historical cost problems we noted earlier.

Net tangible assets

Net tangible assets are the net assets of a company minus its intangible assets. Some analysts use this to help determine the 'true' value of a share, and so whether the current share price is too high or low.

Another ratio that falls under the liquidity banner is interest cover. Interest cover describes how many times the interest expense can be covered by the profits (before interest and tax) of the business. Generally, a higher ratio is better; however, it could also indicate that the company could expand with the use of leverage.

Use of fundamental ratio analysis

Before we leave ratio analysis (only momentarily), it is perhaps worth remembering that, as with all analysis, there are limitations to the effectiveness of ratio analysis. Some of the difficulties arise because there is simply too much data, the data is imperfect, or it may have already been factored in by other market participants rendering it somewhat less than useful for a timely signal to act. Perhaps it will make matters clearer if we say that *fundamentals help determine what, not when, to buy*.

Having an understanding of fundamental ratios is essential to successful long-term investing. For example, there is a high correlation between changes in a company's earnings over more than 10 years and that company's share price.

Understanding the ratios alone, however, is not sufficient for investment success. The successful share trader must be able to demonstrate a method of utilising the information provided by the ratios in a logical, consistent and disciplined manner.

The strategies you develop may fall under several categories — growth, value, contrarian or momentum, or a hybrid of some description. Indeed, for the purposes of diversification, it may make perfect sense to run several strategies simultaneously.

Strategy

We have reached that point now where we can examine strategies used for stock selection. The strategies we will discuss are all focused on finding long-term investment opportunities. As such, the strategies may be subject to the short-term volatility of the market. As discussed earlier, if riding out the short-term volatility of the stockmarket is something you are not comfortable with, you may like to invest in a managed fund.

A strategy is simply a set of carefully researched and selected rules. Rules, established by the individual investor, on what ratios to use, on how to combine them, and when to use them. The rules, however, form only part of the strategy. The investor will also require rules that cover when to sell (if at all), how to weight the portfolio, how to re-weight the portfolio, and when and how to add to the portfolio. Every contingency must be covered.

What should you do if one of the companies you purchased is the target of a takeover? Will you automatically accept the first bid? What will you do with the funds? What will you do with income received from dividends? Will you hold those dividends in cash until some future re-weighting date or will you automatically reinvest? All of these questions require an answer or your strategy cannot be described as 'carefully planned'.

We begin our examination of possible strategies with an example of an approach that attempts to rank companies according to whether they represent good 'value'.

Value investing

Value-based investing is a style where investments are only held as long as they represent good value. The approach can be applied at each stage of the investing process. Even top-down managers, who begin the investment selection process by looking at countries, markets and sectors before looking at the individual company, may determine through the use of various proprietary measures that country A represents better value than country B, that industry A represents better value than industry B and, finally, that company A represents better value than company B. For both top-down managers and bottom-up managers, who start by investigating individual companies, selection is usually based on certain value criteria such as price to earnings, dividend yield, price to cash flow and price to net tangible assets.

Value investing

Value investing is the purchase of securities that are trading significantly below their intrinsic value and, in some cases, selling them when they have risen above their intrinsic value.

Value investing is essentially contrarian in nature. This means that the resultant stocks in the final portfolio are selected contrary to the popular sentiment of the day. For example, if there is enthusiasm for companies that garner much of their profits in Australia, perhaps because the Australian economy is seen as being insulated from a global economic slowdown, companies that generate much of their earnings offshore will be out-of-favour. These companies may see their share prices fall, meaning the dividend yield will rise, and the price/earnings, price to cash flow and price to book value ratios will fall. Because of these lower relative valuations, caused by the majority of investors not 'favouring' this particular company, the stock is viewed as being good value and is purchased.

For further discussion on the efficient market, see Chapter 1.

The value approach also disagrees with some parts of the efficient market concept, while agreeing with it in other parts. In the short term, the market must be inefficient to present value opportunities that are likely to generate above-average returns. In the medium to long term, however, the market must return to efficiency and reflect the true value of the underlying company, meaning the share price will rise.

We know that from time to time markets can misprice companies. This mispricing is often the result of emotions — when emotions are extremely enthusiastic or depressed, prices for companies do not accurately reflect the long-term fundamentals of the company.

There are a large number of value managers in Australia, including those regarded as deep value managers. The philosophy of deep value managers is quite simple and this in turn makes adherence to the proposed strategy easier.

Deep value managers look for stocks that are out of favour with the market but which are predicted to regain favour once the market recognises their 'true value'. Essentially, the managers aim to buy, for example, $1 worth of assets for 60 cents.

Investment process

The investment process for value investing starts by confining the stock 'universe' to a certain number of the largest and most liquid Australian shares that are trading in the most volume, as these are the most readily tradable stocks. The stocks are then compared on a like-for-like basis, looking at such measures as projected balance sheets, profit and loss and cash flows, and valuing the forecast earnings. The managers then forecast a value for the shares at a specified time in the future, calculate the expected investment returns and then rank all the stocks on a daily basis.

Filters are then applied to select a certain number of stocks. This number varies depending on the strategy of the manager.

From the strategies of value managers, a process of stock selection that is simple and that lends itself well to emulation can be developed. This process, for example, could be:

1   Select the most frequently traded 100 companies from the S&P/ASX 200, using trading volume figures.

2   Determine a three-year forecast of intrinsic 'fair value' based on P/E ratio, EPS growth and dividends using historical data.

3   Rank shares according to best relative value.

4   Select the top 25 to 35 for the portfolio.

5   Monitor the investments regularly to ensure they continue to meet requirements and standards.

6   Sell off investments that no longer meet the criteria.

Doing it yourself

There are two ways to build a portfolio based on value investing. The first way is to use a multivariate stock selection process, and this is extremely easy. The other way is to use intrinsic value. This is a little more complex but possibly more accurate. Unfortunately, the second and more complicated method does involve some subjectivity, which by definition is going to be impossible to replicate exactly. Nevertheless, this section is the nuts and bolts of the strategy being examined. For each investment style we look at, this is where we will attempt to replicate the strategies of the country's best managers.

Using the example strategy above, if we forecast a company's value in three years' time, we need to 'discount' the value back to today to obtain a current 'intrinsic' value for the shares. You would need to conduct the same analysis on all of the top 100 companies and then rank them in ascending order — that is, those companies with a share price at the largest discount or smallest premium to their intrinsic value (the cheapest shares) would be at the top of the list, and the companies with the greatest premium (the more expensive shares) at the bottom of the list, as shown in Table 5.1, below.

Table 5.1: Ranking by discount or premium to intrinsic value

Ranking	Share price	Intrinsic value	Discount/premium
1	$1.00	$2.00	Deep discount
2	$2.00	$2.00	Fair value
3	$4.00	$2.00	Premium

Let's examine the steps involved in conducting the analysis ourselves.

Step-by-step calculations

There are many variants of intrinsic value calculations. Here we will examine the simplest method for calculating intrinsic value, using a step-by-step guide to conduct the same stock selection process yourself.

Step 1: gather information

The information you will need to complete our simple intrinsic value calculation includes EPS today, expected EPS growth, dividend payout ratio, historical P/E range and the current expected 10-year bond rate over the next three years.

Step 2: calculate a future value for the shares

The further into the future you forecast, the less accurate your forecast will be. Many analysts forecast earnings for a company for one and two years, and some even go to five. In our example, we will use three years.

Suppose we are trying to forecast the future value for XYZ shares. Through looking at the financial history for company XYZ, we can gather all the information required to calculate this value. From looking at the financials, suppose we find the following information. As at 30 June 2004, XYZ shares had earnings of 30 cents and paid a dividend of 17 cents. This is a payout ratio of 57 per cent, which is lower than the five-year average of about 85 per cent. So let's assume over the next three years the average payout ratio will be 72 per cent. We also find that the company has grown its earnings by 12 per cent in the prior twelve months so let's assume now that the earnings grow conservatively by 5 per cent per year for the next three years. We also know the P/E range the shares have traded at over the last five years — 5.8 times to 24.2 times. (Fund managers, of course, would speak to company management and visit the company to verify some of these numbers. As a private investor you don't usually have that option, so you will need to be more conservative in your estimates to make up for errors in calculations and estimates.)

Using this information, we can calculate a future value for the shares in three years' time based on the expected EPS in 2007 multiplied by a P/E ratio plus the value of the dividends received. To estimate expected EPS over the three years we, in this example, apply our conservative estimate of a 5 per cent growth rate to the 2003–2004 earnings. The expected dividends are then based on a payout ratio of 72 per cent as mentioned earlier. We use a P/E ratio of 8.1 to convert 2007 earnings to a share price equivalent and then add the total dividends to arrive at an expected total value or future share price of $3.53. The calculation is shown in Table 5.2, overleaf.

How did we get 8.1 for the P/E ratio in 2007? We already know that the highest P/E has been 24.2. If we assume that the shares in three years' time are trading at a P/E of 8.1 or one-third of the highest P/E, that would be a conservative assumption.

Table 5.2: Calculating the expected future value of XYZ shares

Year	EPS (Est. 5% growth p.a.)	DPS (EPS × 72% payout ratio)
2004 (Actual)	30	17
2005	31.5	22.7
2006	33.1	23.8
2007	34.7	25.0
	Total dividends for 2005–2007:	71.5

Expected value in 2007 = (EPS × (High P/E ÷ 3)) + Total dividends

= (0.347 × (24.2 ÷ 3)) + 0.715

= (0.347 × 8.1) + 0.715

= $3.53

So from the financial history of XYZ shares, we can forecast a value for the shares in 2007 of $3.53.

Step 3: discount the future value to obtain a fair price for the shares today

Now we simply apply a discounted cash flow or 'present value' formula to the future value to establish a reasonable price to pay for the shares today.

The discounting formula is as shown below.

$$\text{Present value} = \frac{\text{future value}}{(1 + R)^n}$$

In the formula, 'R' equals the current 10-year bond rate plus a few extra percentage points to cover rate rises and 'n' equals the number of years between now and the date of the future value. At the time of writing, the Australian 10-year bond rate is 5.87 per cent. So in this example, using a bond rate of 5.87 per cent plus 5 per cent and 3 as the number of years, we obtain a fair value for XYZ shares of $2.59.

If the share price for XYZ shares was considerably below this level, suggesting the shares were at a discount to their fair value, they would be considered by value investors.

A simpler approach

A simpler approach to value investing is the Australian version of the 'Dogs of the Dow' strategy, originally developed by Michael O'Higgins in the United States.

The steps are:

1 start with the top 50 industrial companies by market capitalisation

2 rank in descending order by dividend yield

3 buy equal dollar amounts of the top 10 ranked companies

4 hold for one or two years and repeat the process.

Investors using this simple strategy have achieved strong returns in the past.

Investing for growth

This chapter will examine growth investing and GARP — or growth at a reasonable price — investing.

Growth managers

As we saw earlier, value investing is a style that can be defined a number of ways — and its proponents afford different weightings to different factors to stand out from one another. In simple terms, however, value investors buy stocks with relatively low P/E, price to book or price to cash flow ratios, or high dividend yields.

Growth managers, on the other hand, assess companies on the basis of their long-term growth potential. They are less concerned about the share price if the growth they predict exceeds that of the company's peers and is therefore expected to result in relative share price overperformance. Growth managers look for companies with high sales and income growth, stable earnings, an efficient use of capital, and high returns on equity, capital and assets. While not actively sought, these sorts of companies generally also have lower dividend yields.

In particular, growth companies are expected to grow irrespective of the economic cycle — often because they

Growth investors

Growth investors' principal aim is to gain earnings growth and achieve capital growth from expected growth in company earnings.

are part of a sector that is growing faster than the general economy, or they have management processes that can be leveraged in the marketplace. Growth candidates may also be new companies in the first part of their product's lifecycle.

A growth manager is generally looking for opportunities to invest in either established or emerging companies within industry sectors that display stronger growth characteristics, including more innovative and speculative industries. Typical examples may include biotechnology, telecommunications, IT, financial services and pharmaceuticals. While growth managers may keep one eye on the P/E ratio, its relevance is somewhat obscured by the above-average rate of growth expected from earnings. In general, growth managers will put more emphasis on earnings growth than on high P/E ratios. Indeed, when we come to the issue of selling a holding, we find many growth managers will sell if the earnings forecasts are not being met. Rarely is a holding sold because the P/E ratio is too high (or too low).

All of this makes growth managers happy to buy stocks at higher prices when they believe the growth story. But growth managers would rarely admit to buying 'overpriced' stocks, just as true value managers would rarely buy an undervalued stock that showed no promise of profit growth.

In practice then, the growth/value line is somewhat blurred and a mix of the two disciplines is often used. Invariably shares are purchased through the use of quantitative models and/or qualitative assessments with little regard as to whether the shares may be categorised as value or growth.

Share price movement particularly in the short term is related to emotions and expectations, which together are referred to as 'sentiment'. This sentiment can mean the same company's shares can appear to be cheap or expensive, depending on the value placed on them by the market at the time. So growth and value managers may own the very same shares — just at different times.

In turn, the different styles create very different performance results — generally, when value investing is performing poorly, growth investing performs well, and vice versa.

While value investing — buying bargains — is popular in Australia, pure growth investing appears to have fewer exponents. Many investment managers such as BT and Colonial First State include growth components as part of their style, but few run pure growth funds. ING, Macquarie Bank and ABN Amro Asset Management each run growth portfolios that appear to more closely resemble a pure growth style, although they too all have some references back to value and price.

Investment process

Growth managers tend to look for opportunities in all sectors, meaning a relative growth comparison will be made in any sector or industry that comes up on their radar.

As they are interested in isolating strong growth companies, growth managers will be largely concerned with one-year earnings per share growth, return on equity, and one-year EPS forecasts. Using these basic screens and quantitative assumptions will not be enough to match a growth manager's portfolio. There are several components where an analyst makes a subjective assessment of the attributes of the potential investment. We cannot replicate this exactly, if at all. However, we can look at some general steps a growth manager may go through when assessing a stock opportunity. The steps are:

1   industry analysis using such tools as a Porter 'five forces' analysis (see below)

2   growth and sustainability screens

3   fundamental company analysis (assessing the strategy, industry position, earnings performance and risk factors of individual companies)

4   quantitative research (analysis of risk and return).

Regarding step three, unless you have some experience in the business the company is in, this can be difficult. We can gain some confidence from the business's performance to date but whether this is likely to continue is another matter. Referring to trade journals, speaking with customers and competitors would all help evaluate the future success for the strategies being implemented but some subjectivity will enter here.

The final step is the analysis of risk and return. Essentially, this is to answer the question of what price to pay.

While we don't know for sure what methods growth managers may use, we can develop some simple models that in essence would have the same effect, as shown below.

Doing it yourself

As we go through the process of attempting to do it ourselves you may notice that to some extent there is a reinventing of the wheel going on. Somebody else is already doing what we are trying to do. Although this may be the case, for the purposes of this example, we need to come up with a model that can be followed relatively easily. As mentioned earlier, replicating a growth manager's model will be difficult as we don't know exactly how individual companies are assessed and we also know that there must necessarily be a high level of subjectivity. There is also a relative-performance component so later we will need to rank the stocks selected and purchase the top relative dozen companies for our own portfolios.

For our purposes, we will outline a step-by-step approach and then examine each step in some detail.

The steps are:

- *Step 1:* determine industries that have excellent growth prospects using a subjective tool such as 'The hill' or Porter's 'five forces' (details to follow). Ensure each company satisfies at least some of the characteristics of sound growth investments, which are:

  - high return on equity

- high return on invested capital
- high profit margin.

■ *Step 2:* for each company that remains in the list (preferably around 30 companies), estimate an earnings growth rate using information supplied by brokers or industry experts.

■ *Step 3:* rank the companies by the PE/G ratio (details to follow) in ascending order — that is, from lowest to highest. Those dozen or so with the lowest PE/G may be selected for the portfolio.

■ *Step 4:* maintain a constant vigil over each of the holdings for the sole purpose of reassessing the growth prospects and watching for any company whose earnings expectations may fall short and thus push its PE/G ratio higher.

Step 1: Assess future growth and sustainability

For ease of analysis, it may be beneficial to invest within the sphere of understanding that you have. For example, if you work in healthcare, you may have a good idea of the companies that are bringing out products you have seen hospitals and health centres purchasing. Alternatively, you may be aware that the socioeconomic changes occurring around you are resulting in a growing demand for an existing product and that there is only one or two suppliers of that product.

However, many growth companies are not established companies but are research and development companies that are hoping to design a new and better product that every business, government or individual will need. The prospects of these products are difficult to assess but nevertheless the rewards for investing early in the next 'hula hoop' can be well worth the effort. The following tools may assist in 'drilling down' to the industries and sectors that have a good chance of growth.

The hill

There are many ways to look at growth and one of the simplest ways is to develop 'themes'. These themes help to explain the sectors that will benefit in the future, in turn helping to isolate the best sectors to focus on for growth investing.

Figure 6.1, below, helps describe the products and the sectors that have boomed and may boom in the future as a result of the spike in the population that occurred after WWII — the baby boomers.

Figure 6.1: The hill

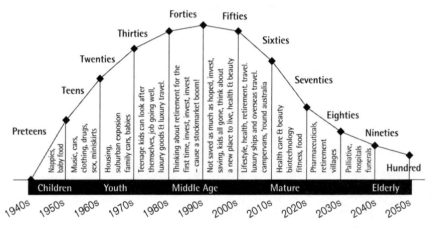

© Roger J. Montgomery, Investors Advantage. Reproduced with permission.

The hill helps a private investor to visualise the life stages of the baby boomers and, in turn, the products or services that will experience growth because of increased demand from this group, depending on what stage of life they are up to.

This tool can be used like the following Porter's 'five forces' to help you start to think about the industries and sectors that are likely to benefit from the changes in baby boomers' future spending habits.

Porter's five forces

Step 1 of our strategy involves an analysis of the industry or sector which the company is within. A useful investor tool for analysing the outlook for a sector or an individual company within that sector, and thus its investment merits, is the Porter 'five forces' framework. This analyses the five underlying factors determining future profitability, as shown in Table 6.1, below and overleaf.

Table 6.1: Porter's five forces

Factor 1: The relative power of suppliers

With powerful and/or large and market-dominating suppliers, it is very difficult to negotiate better prices for supplies. Where it is difficult to negotiate prices with suppliers, cost cutting also becomes difficult. Increasing profit margins is unlikely unless prices for the goods or services being provided can be raised and this depends on the power of the customers. The first question is: Can this business I am looking at force their suppliers to charge less?

Factor 2: The relative power of customers

Are customers forced to buy from the company and forced to pay on time? While customers have little power against utility providers — for example, suppliers of gas and electricity — they have a large amount of power against an online flower seller. Does this business have some pricing power? Can it charge higher prices without incurring protests from its customers and lower sales?

Factor 3: The risk of new entrants

New entrants will invariably reduce the pricing power of the company and therefore erode profit margins. Lower profit margins in turn result in fewer dollars that can be retained to grow the business. A business that has a very strong brand name or one that has a very high natural barrier to entry, such as high setup costs, is certainly a better investment option than a business with low start-up costs that can be quickly replicated. How easy is it to set up and compete effectively with this business?

Factor 4: The risk of substitute products

What are the risks of an alternative product emerging to compete with the current methods, techniques and/or technologies of the company? Obviously, this is very difficult to assess and so there must be some obvious merit in the product or service that demonstrates a robust lifecycle. An alternative product can not only ruin a company, it can decimate an industry — for example, the advent of air travel and its impact on train and sea travel. What is the probability of an alternative product or service emerging?

cont'd

Table 6.1: Porter's five forces

Factor 5: The degree of rivalry

How much rivalry already exists in this industry? A high degree of rivalry is great for consumers but competition is not great for profit margins. A high degree of rivalry also forces a participant to spend a greater proportion of its energy defending its stake, leaving fewer resources available for expanding, diversifying and growing. Is the business winning against its competition and is there too much?

Information derived from: Michael E. Porter, *Competitive strategy: techniques for analysing industries and competitors*, Simon & Schuster Inc, 1980

The same kind of analysis described in Table 6.1 to examine the investment merits of a company can be done for entire industry sectors.

Assuming the company meets Porter's wishlist — that is, the company is a dominant industry player that can control prices of suppliers and the prices it charges consumers without adversely impacting sales and there is little current real competition and it is expensive to set up as an effective competitor — then the next step is to assess the future growth prospects.

Step 2: Estimate earnings growth rate

Once the candidates have been isolated, the next step is to establish reasonable estimates of growth for the companies you have selected. It is prudent to always be conservative in any assumptions that are used to determine an earnings growth rate.

A common question is, 'Where will I get the information to reasonably assess growth potential?' This information can be provided by the analysts at full-service stockbroking firms as well as by online data providers and discount brokers that aggregate 'consensus' numbers — that is, essentially pool together all the forecasts to determine an average.

Step 3: Quantitative assessment

Once you have completed the subjective and qualitative part of the analysis, the difficult work is complete. The next step is to fundamentally analyse and then rank the selected companies. The companies that have been selected may be either established businesses or relatively new entrants. The method we are about to describe accepts both types as candidates and compares their relative price to potential earnings growth.

Building a portfolio of favourites

You should now have a list of companies that have met the discussed criteria — that is, they offer excellent potential growth, either because they fall into an industry that will benefit from exceptional expansion as a result of some theme such as the spikes in demand caused by the baby boomers, or because there is little competition for their product, there is not likely to be any in the future and the industry or company has some power in determining the prices it receives and the prices it pays. It helps to have over 30 companies in this list.

Risk and analysis

Now there is the simple matter of satisfying 'risk and return' analysis. Remember — this step is to ensure that you don't pay too much for growth. You will still want a portfolio of stocks so this step is a ranking process, as the companies are ranked from most desirable to least desirable.

The US investor Peter Lynch, who successfully stewarded the Fidelity funds in the US for 13 years and eclipsed the returns of the S&P 500 there, regularly spoke of 'a 50 per cent grower trading at 25'. While this may initially seem like jargon, he was referring to a company that was growing its earnings at 50 per cent per year but was trading at a P/E ratio of only 25 times.

Lynch hit on the PE/G ratio or the price earnings/growth ratio as a method to assess the price to be paid for growth. The PE/G ratio is determined by dividing the forecast EPS growth by the P/E ratio, in turn determining whether the company is too expensive. The calculation for a hypothetical Company A is shown in Table 6.2, overleaf.

Table 6.2: Calculating the PE/G ratio for 'Company A'

Statistics

EPS 2001 (actual)	35 cents
EPS 2002 (forecast)	48 cents
Current share price	$10.50

Calculations

Forecast EPS growth	(48 − 35) / 35 = 37.15%
P/E ratio	$10.50 / 35 cents = 30 times
PE/G ratio	30 / 37.15 = **0.8076**

Essentially, if the P/E ratio is less than the forecast EPS growth rate, the company will have a PE/G ratio of less than one and be regarded as 'not expensive'. The lower the PE/G ratio, the cheaper the shares are compared to the growth rate being offered. Provided you stick to companies that have a high-expected EPS growth rate, the PE/G can help you rank the best growth stories so that only those that are not 'too expensive' for the growth expected are purchased.

For example, Company A has a PE/G ratio of 0.8077. This means, depending on how that compares to the PE/G ratio you calculate for the other companies in your list, it might be considered a reasonable addition to your portfolio. Execute this formula for each company you selected using the earlier qualitative assessment to rank the companies from lowest to highest PE/G ratio and so choose the best to buy.

Step 4: Monitor your portfolio

Once you have established your portfolio, it is a simple matter of monitoring the EPS growth forecasts for each company and recalculating the PE/G ratios. Changes in the economic environment or dynamics within industry sectors can cause earnings forecasts to be adjusted downwards. If this happens, the stocks should be sold and those that meet the above qualitative analysis and have better PE/G ratios should be purchased.

GARP investing

GARP, or growth at a reasonable price, is an investment style that seeks to combine the merits of both value investing and growth investing.

GARP investors
GARP investors aim to find growth stocks that are selling at a 'cheap' price.

You may recall that value managers look for companies that are cheap. Tyndall (www.tyndall.com.au) in particular looks for companies that are large, established businesses selling below their true or 'intrinsic' value. You may also recall that growth managers look for companies with high earnings growth.

While growth and value managers can appear to be at loggerheads and may argue that their methods are mutually exclusive, for you as an investor the two methods can be complementary.

Growth managers buy stocks that are expected to have strong growth and while the strong growth continues there will be a premium on the share price. A company, however, cannot grow at a rate far in excess of the economic growth rate forever — if it did, it would become the economy. Eventually, the growth rate subsides and the company fails to meet an earnings prediction. The result is a re-rating of the stock and its P/E falls. Growth managers who take no account of price suffer under these circumstances. GARP managers, however, attempt to avoid such a harsh fate by only buying strongly growing companies at cheap prices.

Growth investors are generally willing to pay a premium (certainly higher than value investors) for what they believe to be high quality shares. One of the biggest risks they face is that the growth forecasts for a company may not be met or, even worse, the company may go into a decline that pushes the share price down significantly. Growth portfolios tend to have higher volatility over time than value portfolios, so sharp declines can occur, particularly when growth expectations factored into the company's earnings are not met.

Value shares on the other hand are generally purchased because they are undervalued compared to other companies in the same sector, or compared to some internal aspect of the company such as its book value, the dividend yield or the earnings. There exists a very real risk that the perceived value of the shares may never be realised by the market and the shares remain perpetually undervalued.

Both strategies can go through periods of overperformance and it is often the case that one is performing exceptionally well at precisely the time the other is performing poorly. Each tends to perform in different stages of the economic cycle — growth during and before the bullish expansion phase and value during the maturing phase of the growth part of the economic cycle or during its bear phase. The nice thing about GARP investing is that it is perpetual. It doesn't matter what cycle we are in, companies with the best growth prospects at a cheap price are always prudent investments.

The GARP method is a combination of the growth and value philosophies and perhaps it is a logical extension of the styles already revealed. GARP neatly combines the benefits of growth stocks with the sensible and prudent approach normally associated with value investing. In a nutshell, GARP seeks to buy good quality growth companies cheaply.

In light of this, it seems surprising that exponents of growth and value investing styles are in an intellectual tug-of-war over which approach is the best. As each provides the opportunity for solid returns at different times, there seems to be no need for the debate. It seems more logical to combine the two. Indeed, one might argue that in order to create wealth you must have growth and in order to accelerate that wealth you need to have value. GARP is that strategy.

As we will see later, the only issue that arises now is when to sell. The value and growth styles make the answers to this question quite easy. In pure value investing, the stock is sold if it no longer represents value. In growth investing the shares are sold if the company no longer ranks highly in terms of growth prospects. GARP offers a number of different solutions to this problem and we will explore these later in this chapter.

Why growth is important

Growth in sales and earnings is required to increase the value of a business. Imagine for a moment that a company earned a constant $10 million per year that it distributed to shareholders. This amount never changed and the number of shares on issue remained at a constant 5 million. Valuing the shares becomes very easy — simply divide the dividend per share by the rate of return you would like to receive.

For example, if you wanted an 11 per cent return on your money, you would simply divide the $2.00 per share dividend by 11 per cent and find that the price to pay for the shares is $2.00 ÷ 0.11 = $18.18.

Imagine if all investors wanted the same rate of return. Next year the earnings would be the same and so investors wanting to receive an 11 per cent return would produce a price of $18.18. Indeed, the only thing that may change the price is investors' demands for the rate of return they want to receive. If, for example, interest rates were to rise, investors would necessarily want to receive a higher return and therefore pay a lower price.

Now suppose the company's earnings grew by 10 per cent. In the second year, the earnings would be $2.20 per share and the share price could rise to $20.00 and still give investors an 11 per cent return ($2.20 ÷ 0.11 = $20.00).

So growth in earnings is generally one of the important requirements for a rising share price.

The investment process

GARP investors are looking to invest in stocks which offer an attractive trade-off between growth and value. It is their objective to find underpriced earnings and cash flow in the market. GARP investors will combine such indicators as earnings per share growth and price/earnings ratios to identify stocks. They will also use forecasts of these figures out to five years to ensure that short-term earnings do not obscure longer term growth prospects. GARP investment managers will then use qualitative analysis to determine the longer term growth outlook for the stock. Finally, they will use a particular algorithm to rank the selected stocks.

Doing it yourself

We can closely replicate a GARP investment strategy by using the following three steps:

1   forecast earnings and identify companies with attractive growth prospects

2   combine EPS growth with the P/E ratio

3   translate price for growth scores via algorithm to build portfolio.

Step 1: Forecast earnings and identify companies with attractive growth prospects

One of the key drivers of earnings growth is a high and stable rate of return on equity. So the first step in our version of the GARP investing style is to isolate those companies that have high rates of return on equity. We start our search by looking once again at only large companies — those with market capitalisations over $5 billion. We then remove resource companies and News Corp. The final step is to isolate those companies that generate return on equity in the most recent year of greater than 10 per cent.

Step 2: Combine EPS growth with the P/E ratio

We then seek to calculate the PE/G ratio by dividing each company's forecast EPS growth by its present P/E ratio.

Step 3: Translate price for growth scores via algorithm

Many GARP investment managers will hold 80 to 120 stocks in their portfolio and we are unlikely to replicate this kind of diversification. Besides, the costs are higher and the results more mediocre when so broadly diversified. Our 'algorithm' is a simple 'rank by PE/G ratio in ascending order'. So once we have all the companies listed with all of their PE/G ratios alongside them, we simply rank them from lowest to highest. The five to 10 lowest PE/G ratios become the five to 10 for our portfolio.

While many followers of the PE/G ratio agree that company's shares should only be purchased when the P/E ratio is lower than the forecast EPS growth rate, in order to build a diversified portfolio of 10 shares, you may have to go for the 10 relatively 'cheapest' issues rather than only the 'undervalued' issues.

The process of GARP investing is a sensible one. It is for this reason some growth investors have adopted elements of it — for example, the growth investment example looked at earlier in this chapter used a risk and return analysis filter to ensure the price paid for the growth share was not too high.

Investing for income

Reasons to invest for income

Investing for income can take many forms — from simply placing funds on deposit with a bank or investing in high yielding shares, to using derivatives such as options and instalment warrants to enhance the yield of a portfolio.

Income is seen by many as an important reason to invest in the sharemarket but all investors should be aware for the need for growth in a portfolio to ensure that the purchasing power or income generated is not eroded by inflation. While income is essential, it should not be at the expense of growth.

Consider a hypothetical example that compares shares in a large property development holding company to units in a property trust run by the same organisation.

The holding company shares are trading at $1.00 and offer an initial yield of just 2.5 per cent; however, its share price has grown by an average of 25 per cent per year for the last 10 years. This compares to the property trust units, which are also trading at $1.00. While they offer a yield of 7.5 per cent, they only provide capital growth of 6 per cent per year.

The cash flows and capital gains over 10 years for the shares versus the units are shown in Table 7.1, overleaf.

Table 7.1: Comparing the performance of shares to trust units

| | Shares | | | Trust Units | |
YEAR	Capital	Income	YEAR	Capital	Income
1	$1.00	$0.03	1	$1.00	$0.08
2	$1.25	$0.03	2	$1.06	$0.08
3	$1.56	$0.04	3	$1.12	$0.08
4	$1.95	$0.05	4	$1.19	$0.09
5	$2.44	$0.06	5	$1.26	$0.09
6	$3.05	$0.08	6	$1.34	$0.10
7	$3.81	$0.10	7	$1.42	$0.11
8	$4.77	$0.12	8	$1.50	$0.11
9	$5.96	$0.15	9	$1.59	$0.12
10	$7.45	$0.19	10	$1.69	$0.13
Sub Total	$6.45	$0.83	Sub Total	$0.69	$0.99
Total	$7.28		Total	$1.68	

Despite the higher yield on the property trust units, the lower capital growth has meant that the investor is worse off. Growth is essential in ensuring that the rate of return beats inflation over several years

Suppose you invested $10,000 in the above unit trust with a yield of 7.5 per cent. You would receive income of $750 in the first year. This would compare favourably to the $250 income you would receive if you invested the same amount in the holding company shares. Over 10 years, the total income received from the unit trust would total $9,885. However, because of the shares' greater growth, they would produce total income over 10 years of $8,313. As you can see, the difference in income over 10 years is not as great as might be expected. The real difference is in the capital growth. In this example, the shares have grown by $64,500 compared to the trust units, which have grown by just $6,900. The share portfolio has provided a combined return of $72,819 compared to the property trust units' return of just $16,780.

Inflation

Inflation is the overall increase in the level of prices of goods and services, measured by the Consumer Price Index.

Need to protect against inflation

You also need to consider inflation. With an inflation rate of, for example, 5 per cent per annum, inflation will erode the purchasing power of a fixed income by half in just 10 years and by half again in 15 years.

For example, putting $500,000 into a term deposit yielding a fixed 7 per cent would produce $35,000 income per year. After 10 years, this income would be eroded by a 5 per cent inflation rate to just $20,955 in real dollars.

An alternative is to put $500,000 into the stock market. At a conservative dividend yield of, say, 3 per cent, this would produce income of $15,000 in the first year. But the stockmarket grows over time and over 20 years it is reasonable to conservatively expect 8 per cent growth. In the fifteenth year, the income produced by the portfolio would be approximately $70,000. The income itself has grown at 8 per cent, easily keeping up with inflation. More impressive, however, is the growth in the portfolio. The $500,000 has grown to $2.3 million after 15 years compared to the term deposit which remains at $500,000.

While income is an important part of the total return to an investor, it is imperative to have growth. This is certainly a different message to that which is traditionally told to certain people — for example, retirees who are told that as you get older, you need more income. Given that a retiree today could reasonably expect to live at least another 20 years, it is still important to seek growth. Going straight into property trusts and term deposits, as the above examples show, may not always be the best course of action.

Nevertheless, there are tax advantages available to investors who pursue income produced by companies upon which tax is already paid, as you will see in the following.

Dividend imputation

The introduction of dividend imputation by the Australian government in 1987 was an attempt to improve the equitable distribution of company earnings. Previously, company profits were taxed twice when distributed to a shareholder. Under the old system, after a company paid tax on its profits and subsequently distributed part of these after-tax profits as a dividend, the individual shareholders were taxed on that part of the after-tax profits distributed to them.

Dividend imputation means that when a shareholder is liable to pay tax on dividend income, he or she is effectively allowed a tax credit for the tax that the company has already paid on the profits from which the dividend was paid.

Depending on the amount of tax the company has paid, what franked dividends it received itself, whether income was generated offshore and other components of the company's tax situation, dividends may be fully franked, partially franked or unfranked.

Franked simply means there is a tax credit attached to the dividend, which effectively represents the tax the company has already paid. A fully franked dividend means that the whole dividend carries a tax credit at the applicable company tax rate. This provides the maximum benefit of dividend imputation to shareholders. Unfranked dividends are those to which no tax credits apply.

Most large industrial companies pay enough tax to be able to attach a full tax credit to their dividends — in other words, the dividends are fully franked. A company's individual circumstances, however, can result in changes to the level of tax credits available. A company is allowed to claim many expenses against its income including losses from previous years carried forward. The result is that the full rate of tax is not paid on the company's earnings. This may mean that not enough tax has been paid to ensure that a tax credit can be attached to the entire dividend paid to shareholders and as a result only part of the dividend is franked and the other portion is unfranked.

Benefits for the investor

The benefit of franked and partially franked dividends to an individual shareholder depends on the investor's own taxable income and marginal tax rate.

If the marginal tax rate of the investor is higher than the company tax rate at which the tax credits have been calculated, the investor will have to pay tax only to the extent needed to make up the difference between their marginal rate and the company rate.

If the investor's marginal and/or average tax rate is less than the appropriate company rate, not only will the investor pay no tax on the franked dividend, but he or she will also have an unused credit. This credit can be used to offset tax that would otherwise have to be paid on other income.

Finally, if the investor's taxable income is too low to make him or her liable to tax, or the franking credit exceeds the overall tax liability, the investor will be entitled to receive a refund from the Australian Taxation Office for any excess franking credit.

The net result of the dividend imputation process is that the tax paid by most investors on their dividend income is less than the tax on an equivalent level of income from other investments such as term deposits and fixed-interest securities. And in addition to this tax-advantaged income, there remains the possibility of capital gain.

As a shareholder, you must declare as income not just the cash dividend but the tax credit as well. Table 7.2, below, shows the before-tax and after-tax yield of a fully franked dividend received by an investor paying a marginal tax rate of 47 per cent (excluding the Medicare Levy). The investor owns 10,000 shares purchased for $10 each and receives a fully franked dividend of 35 cents per share. The company tax rate is 30 per cent.

Table 7.2: Calculating dividend yields for an investor paying 47% tax

Franked dividend received [A]	$3,500
Imputation credit (non-cash)	$1,500
Total assessable income	$5,000
Tax at 47%	$2,350
Less franking credit offset	$1,500
Net tax payable [B]	$850
After-tax return [A] – [B]	$2,650
Before-tax yield ($3,500 / $100,000)	3.50%
After-tax yield ($2,650 / $100,000)	2.65%

Note: the Medicare Levy is payable on the total assessable income amount of $5,000.

As you can see from Table 7.2, the after-tax yield (excluding the Medicare levy) to the investor is 2.65 per cent. Compare this to the same income received from an interest-bearing investment such as a term deposit. $3,500 interest income on a $100,000 deposit would have the same before-tax yield of 3.50 per cent. But the after-tax yield for an investor paying a marginal tax rate of 47 per cent (excluding the Medicare levy) would be just 1.70 per cent.

Instead of comparing after-tax yields, which are affected by the investor's marginal tax rate and the application of the Medicare levy, you can compare the before-tax yields of two investments by 'grossing up' the dividend yield to reflect the value of the imputation credit. For example, the grossed-up dividend yield for the shares in Table 7.2 would be calculated as shown below.

$$\text{grossed-up yield} = \frac{(\text{dividend} + \text{imputation credit})}{\text{amount invested}}$$

$$= \frac{(\$3,500 + \$1,500)}{\$100,000}$$

$$= 5.00\%$$

The above grossed-up dividend yield of 5.00 per cent can be compared to the before-tax yield of 3.50 per cent on the term deposit.

Holding period rule

An investor's ability to apply franking credits to offset his or her tax liability may be affected by the 'holding period rule' under the taxation legislation.

The holding period rule applies to shareholders whose total franking tax offsets for the year from all franked dividends received either directly or indirectly through partnerships or trusts exceed the threshold of $5,000. In most cases, such shareholders must own the shares for at least 45 days (not counting the day of acquisition or disposal) after the shares go ex dividend before being entitled to a franking tax offset. If the shares are preference shares, the shareholder must hold them for more than 90 days.

Ex dividend

Ex dividend shares entitle the seller to a dividend that has been declared but not yet paid.

Dividend imputation funds

Dividend imputation funds are simply investment trusts which invest in a high proportion of shares paying franked dividends. To benefit fully from dividend imputation, the investor needs to be paying income tax and generally (as we demonstrated earlier) the investor should be comfortable with slightly higher volatility in return for potentially higher growth. Finally, the investor should generally consider at least a five-year time frame for the investment to be successful.

When a fund invests in Australian shares that pay franked dividends, it can use the imputation credits to offset any resultant tax liability for the members of the fund. For example, suppose a fund has generated interest income of $100,000 and $35,000 of dividend income, which is fully franked at the 2004–2005 company tax rate of 30 per cent. This means that in addition to the interest and dividend income, the fund would have received non-cash imputation credits of $15,000. This amount can be distributed along with the dividends and interest to members of the fund and used to reduce their tax liability accordingly.

Many fund managers offer imputation funds that strive to take advantage of both growth and franked dividends. As already mentioned, the amount of imputation credits available to the investor will be dependent on the amount of Australian tax paid by the company, and also on whether the investors have held their units in the fund for more than 45 days (unless total imputation credits do not exceed $5,000).

Investing can have differing effects on taxation, depending on your circumstances. You should consult with a licensed taxation adviser regarding the effects on your situation.

Investment process

Many fund managers investing for high income returns employ the following strategy:

- look at a wide range of shares and other securities, chosen for their fundamental value

- rate shares on the basis of prospective earnings, the business cash flow, gross dividend yield and other appropriate measures
- favour shares providing imputation credits
- allow cash to play an important part of the investment strategy by reducing the volatility of the investment results.

Doing it yourself

Any of the previous strategies covered in Chapters 5 and 6 can be modified to become a self-managed 'imputation fund'.

As an example, suppose the value approach outlined in Chapter 5 is followed. Rather than selecting the top 10 net dividend yielding shares, the franking is taken into account to provide a 'gross' dividend figure. This ensures that not only is the dividend taken into account but also the proportion of the dividend that is franked. The shares would then be ranked by the grossed-up dividend yield and provide the investor with a group of companies that offer a very high 'relative' level of franked dividends.

Using derivatives for extra income or a higher yield

Many professional investors utilise derivatives to enhance the yield on their portfolios or to achieve a cheaper entry price on the shares they wish to purchase. For example, extra income can be generated over and above dividends by writing call options against the shares being held. By writing options investors receive the option premium upfront. The strategy is not risk free, however — for example, if the shares rise sufficiently in price, they may be called away by the buyer of the option. Another strategy is to buy instalment warrants.

Example — instalment warrants

Another alternative, and one gaining significant investor support, is instalment warrants. Put simply, an instalment warrant is similar to buying a product on hire purchase. Those advertisements for consumer goods that provide an opportunity to 'pay half now and half later' effectively captures the essence of the instalment warrant — although instalments can have a variety of gearing levels from 40 per cent up to 95 per cent.

In simple terms, instalments are a loan to buy shares without the obligation to repay the loan nor the risk of receiving margin calls. Instalment warrants can offer a higher yield and, importantly, the growth element that we highlighted as essential earlier. With instalment warrants, the purchaser, even though he or she has only paid for half of the share, receives the right to all the dividend payments and franking credits as if the shares were owned outright. Additionally, given some of the instalment value is a borrowing cost, there may be some tax advantages as well. Table 7.3, below, shows a hypothetical instalment warrant purchase.

Table 7.3: Hypothetical instalment warrant purchase

Example: Instalment warrant XYZ

ASX code:	XYZGIB
Underlying:	XYZ shares
Share price:	$16.50
1st instalment:	$7.20 (incl. 80¢ interest)
2nd instalment:	$11.50 (incl. 90¢ interest)
Borrowing fee:	$0.43 (part of first instalment)
Total cost:	$7.20 + $11.50 = $18.70
Maturity:	26 June 2006
Issuer:	Australia's first bank

The main advantage of the instalment warrant is the leverage associated with the purchase. By outlaying a smaller amount of capital, a similar exposure to the market can be obtained. In the above example, if the underlying shares rose by $2.00, the gain in percentage terms would equate to 12.12 per cent. The same gain on the instalment price, would equate to a 26.6 per cent return.

Leverage also results in a higher yield. Suppose XYZ shares paid a dividend yield of 3.5 per cent, or a total dividend of 57 cents per share. The same dividend would be paid to the instalment warrant holder, meaning the insalment holder would receive a yield of 7.91 per cent. The warrant holder would obtain the full benefit of the franking credit and also may be able to receive the benefit of a tax deduction for the interest component of the instalment payment.

The downside is that the leverage works against the investor if the shares fall in value. A further possible negative is the premium paid for the instalment. The previous example shows a share price of $16.50, but the total value of purchasing the shares through instalment warrants would be $18.70, or $2.20 more. Provided the shares rise in value, this additional cost may actually prove beneficial through the possible tax deduction of the borrowing costs. If the shares trade sideways or lower, however, the borrowing cost will erode the premium value of the warrant.

> For more information about warrants, talk to ASX Investor Education about the range of derivatives courses available. Also check the ASX website (www.asx.com.au).

Selling options for income

Another popular strategy to enhance the income component of a portfolio is to sell options against stock that is held and receive the premium from selling the option. This premium increases the total return on the portfolio. An investor may also buy shares and write options against them and, if the shares move sideways to slightly higher by the expiry date of the options, a greater return is generated than if the only the shares were purchased.

> **Options**
>
> A call option gives the holder the right but not the obligation to buy the underlying security at a specified price within a certain period of time.
>
> A put option gives the holder the right but not the obligation to sell the underlying security at a specified price within a certain period of time.

In this chapter we offer a brief taste of some of the yield enhancing strategies available through using options. However, there are many subtle variations in option strategies and outcomes that each present different risk profiles. As such, the interested investor should seek further information and perhaps consider attending the derivatives courses run by ASX.

Example — buy and write

A 'buy and write' is the simultaneous writing (or selling) of a call option and the purchase of the equivalent number of shares over which the option will be written. When implementing buy and writes it is common for traders to forget that they may end up holding the stock if the price does not rise. Be sure that you are happy to hold the stock if you are not exercised on the written call.

Another important consideration is that no matter how far the share price rises, the buyer-writer will make no more than the premium received for writing the call plus the difference between the share price paid and the exercise/ strike price of the option (or less the difference if the option was at the money or in the money when written).

The best of both worlds occurs if the shares rise moderately in price and the options expire without having been exercised.

Table 7.4, below, shows a strategy where shares are bought for $4.00 and a $5.00 call option is sold for $0.20. The potential profit or loss to the investor is affected by the share price on the expiry date of the option.

At the money
An option is at the money if the exercise price of the contract is equal to the current market price of the underlying security.

In the money
A call option is in the money if the exercise price is below the current market price of the underlying security.

Table 7.4: Buy and write profit or loss at expiry — shares purchased at $4.00

Share price at expiry	Sold $5.00 call 20c	Total profit / loss
$2.50	$0.20	($1.30)
$3.00	$0.20	($0.80)
$3.50	$0.20	($0.30)
$4.00	$0.20	$0.20
$4.50	$0.20	$0.70
$5.00	$0.20	$1.20
$5.50	($0.50)	$1.20
$6.00	($1.00)	$1.20
$6.50	($1.50)	$1.20

Remember the definition of an option. The buyer has purchased the right but not the obligation to exercise. If you were to write an in the money option, it is likely you will be exercised by the buyer (but not always).

In Table 7.4, you can see that, as the price rises, the maximum profit is $1.20. Even if the shares were to rise to $20.00, the buyer of the call option (not you) will exercise his or her right to buy the shares at $5.00. You as the buyer-writer will be obligated to deliver the shares at $5.00. As you originally purchased the shares at $4.00, you will lock in a $1.00 profit on the shares and the 20 cents premium from the option — that is, a total profit of $1.20.

In these circumstances an investor who would prefer to keep his or her position in the stock will be disadvantaged by having to forgo the price rise by virtue of being short the call option. However, an investor who is only interested in collecting the time premium on the option will not be unduly worried about this situation. An investor who does not wish to have the stock called away will have to close out the option position at a loss.

If by contrast the price of the stock falls, the buyer-writer will lose. The only difference is that 20-cent premium on the written option provides a downside buffer. Buying the stock at $4.00 and writing an option to receive 20 cents indicates that a loss won't be incurred until the stock falls below $3.80. The ideal circumstances for a buy and write is a neutral or slightly bullish market. If there has been a large number of investors writing naked calls, they may rush to cover stock called away by the exercise of their options and this could cause a short-term spike in the price.

Covered writing has great appeal because it reduces the risk of holding stock and reduces the volatility of your shareholding or portfolio. There are risks, however, and the investor must be careful to ensure as far as possible that enough income is being earned to compensate for those risks. Writing covered calls on a stock that has low volatility will result in little income being earned, because the premium on the call option will be lower. This lower income may not be enough to offset the risk of missing out on capital gains and the transaction costs associated with implementing the strategy.

Example — protected buy and write

A protected buy and write is a strategy that attempts to overcome the perceived risk of the shares falling in price. This risk is offset by taking (buying) an out of the money put option. Because taking a put adds extra cost to the

Naked and covered calls

Naked calls are where the writer of the call option does not own the underlying shares which would be necessary for settlement.

Covered calls are where the underlying shares are owned by the writer of the option.

strategy and consequently reduces its potential profit, an out of the money put places the least pressure on the profit earnings capacity of the strategy.

The true benefits of the strategy become apparent if there is a substantial decline in the price of the shares that have been purchased. The strategy has also been referred to as a 'long box' conversion and its payoff diagram is simply a horizontal line. It is a type of spread and is known as a locked trade because the value at expiry is totally independent of the price of the underlying instrument. If you can buy the strategy at a lower price than the value at expiry, there is a profit.

Payoff diagram
A payoff diagram depicts the profit and loss structure of an option.

Suppose we buy 1,000 shares at $5.00. We then write a June $5.00 call at 40 cents, and then take one June $4.50 put at 17 cents. The total cost of the strategy is shown below.

1,000 shares at $5.00	-$5,000
June $5.00 call at 40 cents	+$400
June $4.50 put at 17 cents	-$170
Total cost of the strategy	**$4,770**

Table 7.5, below, illustrates the payoff (profits and losses) at different share prices for the strategy we have just described.

Table 7.5: Protected buy and write strategy — profit and loss

Share Price At Expiry	Stock Profit (Loss)	June $5.00 Call Profit (Loss)	June $4.50 Put Profit (Loss)	Total Profit (Loss)
$3.50	-$1.50	+$0.40	$+0.83	-$0.27
$4.00	-$1.00	+$0.40	$+0.33	-$0.27
$4.50	-$0.50	+$0.40	$-0.17	-$0.27
$5.00	-$0.00	+$0.40	$-0.17	-$0.27
$5.50	+$0.50	-$0.10	$-0.17	+$0.23
$6.00	+$1.00	-$0.60	$-0.17	+$0.23
$6.50	+$1.50	-$1.10	$-0.17	+$0.23
$7.00	+$2.00	-$1.60	$-0.17	+$0.23

The benefits of the strategy can be seen when it is compared to the same buy and write that is unprotected (that is, no put option is purchased for protection), shown in Table 7.6, overleaf.

Table 7.6: Same buy and write strategy — unprotected profit and loss

Share Price At Expiry	Stock Profit (Loss)	June $5.00 Call Profit (Loss)	Total Profit (Loss)
$3.50	-$1.50	+$0.40	-$1.10
$4.00	-$1.00	+$0.40	-$0.60
$4.50	-$0.50	+$0.40	-$0.10
$5.00	-$0.00	+$0.40	+$0.40
$5.50	+$0.50	-$0.10	+$0.40
$6.00	+$1.00	-$0.60	+$0.40
$6.50	+$1.50	-$1.10	+$0.40
$7.00	+$2.00	-$1.60	+$0.40

The first thing you may notice is that the protected buy and write has a lower maximum profit; however, unlike the unprotected buy and write, the protected buy and write has a maximum loss. The unprotected buy and write has potentially unlimited losses (until the stock falls to zero).

The protected buy and write is seldom used because you don't normally expect a heavy fall in the share price. You wouldn't initiate a buy and write if you thought the market was going to fall significantly (you'd just buy a put). Because of the lower risk, however, the protected buy and write may be a worthy way for new investors to introduce themselves to the practice of writing covered calls.

For more information on options, see *Trading options — the ASX way*.

As mentioned, options strategies and warrant strategies are an advanced topic and investors should seek further advice before undertaking specific strategies.

Ethical investing

The concept of socially responsible investment, or 'ethical' investment, has entered the consciousness of mainstream investors. Quite simply, ethical investing involves the analysis of the 'triple bottom line' — not only analysing financial performance, but also environmental and social performance before making an investment decision.

Social investing, socially responsible investing, socially aware investing, ethical investing and mission-based investing all describe the same concept. These terms are all used to describe an investing approach that brings together or integrates social and environmental concerns.

Socially responsible investors are those individuals, businesses, universities, hospitals, foundations, pension funds, religious institutions and other non-profit organisations that consciously put their money to work in ways designed to achieve their financial goals while also working to achieve non-financial goals such as social reform, environmental policy improvements and even improved human rights. Ethical investing requires investment managers to add an additional layer of qualitative analysis of corporate policies, practices and impacts to the traditional quantitative analysis of profit potential. No longer does the investor simply ask if management is the most efficient employer of capital.

Each investor has a different idea of what constitutes an ethical or socially responsible investment. Some investors refrain from purchasing shares in companies that sell tobacco, or shares in wine and gaming companies; others see these companies as merely catering to consumers' needs and prefer to avoid mining companies because of their poor environmental records. Or there are some investors who believe certain mining companies have a better environmental record than others and so rate them by that.

Socially responsible investing is the name for an investment approach that encompasses three main strategies:

- positive screening
- negative screening
- shareholder advocacy.

Each strategy works to promote socially and environmentally responsible business practices which, in turn, contribute to improvements in the quality of life throughout society.

'Screening' in this context is the practice of including or excluding shares from investment portfolios based on the selected socially responsible criteria. Shareholder advocacy is the process of requesting change by a company through talking with the company on issues of concern, and submitting and voting on proxy resolutions. Socially responsible proxy resolutions are aimed at influencing corporate behaviour toward a more responsible level of corporate citizenship, and steering management toward action that enhances the wellbeing of all the company's stakeholders.

Table 8.1, opposite, shows the types of screens used by American fund managers in 2003 to filter out companies that engaged in socially undesirable activities. Out of a total of $2,164 billion involved in socially and environmentally responsible investing, the amount invested in each screen type is also shown.

Table 8.1: Mutual fund screen types

Screen type	Total assets ($billions)
Tobacco	124
Alcohol	93.4
Labour relations	31.1
Environment	28.9
Gambling	28.8
Defence/weapons	23.8
Equal employment opportunity	22
Products/services	16.6
Human rights	11.2
Community impact	10.3
Other	14.1

Ethical investing began during the series of social and environmental movements that developed during the 1960s and 1970s. These concerns soon widened to include management and labour issues. As new information about issues such as global warming, ozone depletion and working conditions in factories around the world become available, combined with incidents such as Chernobyl and the Exxon Valdez disaster, socially responsible investing has become more widespread.

How does it work?

Listed companies are trying to convince investors and the new ethical funds that they recognise their broader responsibilities in society and take into account environmental and social issues when making decisions.

Ethical investing, however, is not, as they say in the US, all beer and skittles. There are no standards for what is ethical and what is not, and many fund managers who are expert at picking stocks do not have the background or expertise to decide what is good corporate social behaviour.

For this reason, there is a new group of analysts who don't look at the financials of a company but rate them based on their social desirability. For the listed companies concerned, this raises the spectre of more scrutiny and more analysis.

Organisations called 'green gatekeepers' are now being set up to service the fund managers who want to know whether a company they may wish to invest in is socially suitable — or a 'socially responsible investment' (SRI). These organisations tend to present the facts for investors to digest. Green gatekeepers conduct exhaustive and detailed research about a company's ethical performance. Information may be collected from many sources including company reports, documents and questionnaires, as well as government and media reports, and court decisions. Government agencies and environmental and union organisations may also be consulted.

Analysis process and methods

The analysis process begins when an ethical investor approaches a researcher with guidelines setting out the type of companies they wish to invest in. The research firm then checks the guidelines against its databases and suggests companies that fit the client's principles.

In Australia there are three main methods investors use to determine an SRI. The most popular, perhaps because it is the easiest, is negative screening, in which companies are excluded from being an SRI for a variety of reasons, including their environmental records, their products or their company policies.

Negative screening excludes all stocks operating in certain industries, such as tobacco or gambling, or, for example, any company that unnecessarily:

- pollutes land, air or water
- discriminates by way of race, religion or sex in employment, marketing or advertising practices
- destroys or wastes non-renewable resources.

The conventional approach is to apply a screen to the universe of companies, typically to eliminate those involved in alcohol, tobacco, gaming, armaments and other activities deemed unacceptable. Normal investment principles are then applied.

Another method is called positive screening and involves seeking out those companies that have a good environmental or social record, such as companies that are involved in developing sustainable energy sources, have a good philanthropic record or have equitable industrial relations policies.

A positive screen would be actively looking, for example, for companies that provide for and support:

- development of sustainable land use and food production

- alleviation of poverty in all forms

- dignity and wellbeing of animals.

Under positive screening, companies are selected based on criteria that may include a company's corporate governance standards, its commitment to sustainable environmental practices or its ownership of technology that could solve environmental problems. The aim of a positive screening approach is to encourage better corporate behaviour, rather than punish companies for their failure to meet certain criteria.

Another method is the 'best of sector' approach, which allows SRI investors to invest in, for example, mining or tobacco stocks by selecting the 'least worst'. While this aids diversification, some experts argue this approach allows companies with poor environmental or poor ethical records to be viewed as an ethical investment.

The use of ratings is another controversial issue in the SRI community because of the subjectivity involved. For example, do you invest in a company that stops logging old-growth forests but has been convicted in the past of anti-competitive pricing behaviour? Do you invest in a company that has improved its mining process in preference to a manufacturer of food rations for third-world countries that produces pollutants during that manufacturing process?

Some researchers use rating systems but this also assumes that the research firm has been able to get the same information from every company, which is difficult if not impossible. While a lot of information is made public via annual reports, ASX announcements and through the media, capturing all this news and weighing it up against what other companies are doing is the difficult part of the process and the results of the screenings are a function of community attitudes which can change significantly over time.

Another screening approach is to focus on companies that are perceived to contribute directly to environmental and socially sustainable economic activity, such as companies involved in renewable energy, recycling, waste management and health care. This 'industries of the future' approach may result in a heavy weighting of funds to smaller companies and a high level of risk, such as exposure to 'new economy' industries if those are viewed as being environmentally sound.

The majority of investment managers use multiple screens for their screened portfolios. A study by the Social Investment Forum (SIF) in the United States found that about a third of the managers listed in the 1997 Nelson's Directory of Investment Managers identify themselves as running portfolios with social screens and 88 per cent of these managers employ three or more screens.

Social advocacy

Then there is 'shareholder activism' or as we mentioned earlier, social advocacy. Using this strategy, the investor can build a portfolio with large ethical constraints but will closely monitor the actions of the companies in the portfolio according to ethical criteria. If a company acts contrary to the criteria, the fund manager will try to apply pressure on that company's management to improve or modify its behaviour.

The impact of socially responsible investing

The effect of having a good corporate record is obvious. A small group of companies meet the various criteria and a large pool of ethical funds must invest in them. The P/E ratio of these companies must rise as they are purchased. Despite corrections and volatility, the market is valuing smaller alternative energy stocks more highly than the established old fuel providers.

The following are examples of changes to corporate practice that have occurred in the US and Australia due to SRI:

■ In 2002, after pressure from investors and environmental groups, Staples announced it would increase the post-consumer recycled and alternative fibre content in its paper products to 30 per cent. The company also plans to phase out selling paper derived from endangered forests.

■ After one year of talks with shareholders, Baxter International, the world's largest healthcare products manufacturer, agreed to look for alternatives and to phase out polyvinyl chloride (PVC) materials in its intravenous products. During manufacture and incineration, PVCs release dioxin. Two hospital corporations — Universal Health Services and Tenant Healthcare — also agreed to research alternatives to PVCs.

■ RJ Reynolds agreed to separate its tobacco business from its food business, which shareholders had encouraged the company to do for years.

■ After many years of significant pressure from investors, as of August 2003, 93 companies of the Fortune 100 had sexual orientation non-discrimination policies.

■ Several green shareholder groups involved with companies such as BHP-Billiton, Boral and Wesfarmers have tried for many years to change company attitudes to environmental issues. These groups are starting to see results and are now able to influence management. One such shareholder group wrote to BHP's chairman asking him to allow some small magnetite leases in environmentally sensitive areas to lapse. They were allowed to lapse. One of the leaders of a group poignantly remarked to a newspaper journalist, 'I don't want my dividends coming at the expense of people on the Fly River'.

A further change to corporate practice is that issuers of investment products in Australia are required to disclose the 'extent to which labour standards or environmental, social or ethical considerations are taken into account in the selection, retention or realisation of the investment' by corporations law.

How popular is it?

Ethical investing is gaining popularity and where previously fund managers were trying to push their products on financial planners, it is now the investors who are demanding this choice. A study released by Corporate Monitor in March 2004 showed the ethical investment sector in Australia increased by more than 20 per cent in the second half of 2003 to $2.8 billion. The biggest ethical investors are the charitable trusts (within the religious sector).

What sorts of returns can be achieved?

A study released by Corporate Monitor in August 2004 found for the year to 30 June 2004 ethical funds returned, on average, 22.27 per cent while mainstream funds returned 16 per cent. For the three years to 30 June 2004 the annualised return for ethical funds was 8.52 per cent and 1.5 per cent for mainstream funds. For the five years to 30 June 2004 the ethical funds returned, on average, 11.67 per cent while the mainstream funds returned 5.7 per cent.

Michael Walsh, executive director of Corporate Monitor, argued the increased returns had been caused by the ethical funds' focus on small companies, which have had strong growth in the past five years, and on companies such as those operating in the alternative energy industry or biotechnology, which have bounced back strongly after the tech boom and bust of the late 1990s and 2000. Walsh also acknowledged that, because of this focus on small companies, ethical funds' returns tend to be more volatile than the returns of mainstream funds.[1]

Difficulties

From an individual investor's perspective, it may be quite easy to build a well-balanced investment portfolio that excludes industries such as tobacco, alcohol or uranium mining, but obtaining proper diversification can become difficult depending upon your beliefs.

As discussed, differing opinions on what constitutes 'ethical' can make it difficult for investors to be sure their funds are being invested as they would like. The difficulties are highlighted when we look at two ethical managers.

Australian Ethical Investments (AEI), an established ethical fund manager, does not hold shares in any of the big four banks. Back in 1997, AEI was a shareholder in the Bank of Melbourne but was forced to accept Westpac's share swap takeover offer. AEI was not happy holding Westpac shares — perhaps because they may lend to companies that could use the funds in ways that harm the environment — and so sold them. But at the time Westpac promoted itself as an ethical fund manager. Westpac Investment Management ran the Australian Eco Share Fund, which the bank claimed was one of the industry's leading ethical funds.

Australian ethical investors

The number of mainstream ethically managed funds in Australia is growing and at the time of writing there were 15 retail ethical investment trusts on offer — including those offered by Glebe Asset Management, Australian Ethical

---

1   Source: Collett, John. Ethical funds, 4 August 2004; cited on moneymanager.smh.com.au/articles.

Investments, AMP Capital Investors, Perennial Investment Partners, Hunter Hall Investment Management, Tower Australia, Perpetual Investments and BT Financial Group among others.

Doing it yourself

There are two simple approaches that can be adopted to build an ethical portfolio — negative screening and positive screening. Obviously, the screening process must be applied using your own criteria. We cannot do this for you.

Negative screening

The steps to negatively screen companies for ethical investment are as follows:

1   Conduct value or growth analysis.

2   Narrow the universe of stocks to 15 using normal financial constraints such as fundamental ratios or performance criteria.

3   Examine in detail the corporate practices and activities of each company and its directors.

4   Remove those that don't satisfy you from an ethical or social responsibility standpoint.

Positive screening

The steps to positively screen companies for ethical investment are as follows:

1   Isolate companies that have positive human rights, animal welfare and environmental track records. Include all companies that you feel meet your own social responsibility requirements from a qualitative perspective (at this stage, don't worry about the financials). The companies you have selected become your 'universe'. It is from this group that your ultimate portfolio will be constructed.

2   Conduct analysis on these companies as you would for growth, value or GARP.

3   Isolate the best performers from this analysis.

4   Hold these companies until they fail the financial criteria, no longer meet the ethical tests or a new company satisfies the criteria more convincingly.

Market neutral investing

In today's volatile markets, managing risk is more important than ever. Investors are looking for downside protection while maintaining good returns — and market neutral investing has become one of the hottest methods to meet that need. Market neutral investments are attractive because they have produced substantially better risk-adjusted returns than the market during the past 10 years. However, the complexities created by the combination of longs, shorts, and leverage make market neutral strategies very different from conventional investments.

The main objective of a market neutral style of investment is to minimise market and sector risk. This is achieved by buying stocks which are expected to outperform the market and short selling stocks which are expected to underperform the market.

Short selling involves selling stocks that you do not yet own. You stand to make a profit if the share price falls before you buy the same stock back. The ASX allows short selling of approved stocks only and certain conditions and restrictions apply. In particular, the settlement date must be no more than 10 trading days after the date of sale and the seller must provide an initial margin to cover at least

Short selling
Short selling is the practice of selling a security that is borrowed but not yet owned, in the expectation of buying the security later (in order to repay the lender) at a lower price and making a profit.

20 per cent of the contract price. Calls will be made for additional margin cover if the price of the short sold shares rises by more than 10 per cent.

The goal of market neutral investing is to make positive investment returns in a down market as well as in an up market. Theoretically, when long and short positions are equally weighted and securities are paired for each sector, the market neutral style should render the portfolio insensitive to market risk. Pairing of stocks is done to match long and short positions for each sector separately to attempt to cancel out risk associated with each position.

How it works

Market neutral investing is a difficult concept to grasp as it involves taking both bought and sold positions in the market so that effectively the direction of the market has a nil effect on profits. Admittedly it sounds a little obscure but market neutral investing requires positions in the market to be offset by opposite positions that cancel out the exposure to the broad market direction, hence the name market neutral.

In its broadest sense, market neutral investing involves taking positions in a market while ensuring that the total portfolio has no net exposure to that market. There are a number of different definitions of market neutral, such as 'no net cash exposure', 'no net beta exposure', 'no net duration exposure', and 'zero market correlation'. A market neutral manager will generally hold both long and short positions but may impose additional constraints (such as no net country or currency exposure for a global portfolio, or no net sector exposure for a domestic portfolio).

Most market neutral investing has been done through long-short equity strategies. Typically, an investor buys undervalued stocks chosen through a quantitative selection process and sells short an equivalent amount of overvalued stocks. Returns derive from the stock purchased and the interest on the short sale proceeds. As long as the long portfolio outperforms the short, the yield over money market rates is positive. Indeed equity investors want to earn a profit greater than the risk-free rate, usually defined as three-month bank bills, whether or not their respective markets move up or down.

The mechanics

We will set out the mechanics of market neutral investing under four different sharemarket scenarios, as shown in Table 9.1, overleaf. In the first instance, before each scenario unfolds, let's assume the investor implemented the following position:

- buys 1,000 shares in ABC at $2.00, paying $2,000
- short sells 1,000 shares in XYZ at $4.00, receiving $4,000
- deposits $4,000 into bank bills paying interest at 8 per cent per annum.

As can be seen from Table 9.1, provided the share purchase outperforms the short sale in any direction, a return greater than the money market should accrue.

Although market neutrality is in itself an interesting characteristic, there are other valuable aspects of the market neutral approach — the freedom in shorting unattractive assets and the opportunity to leverage excess returns. In a simple example, we will demonstrate the additional flexibility a manager has by using a market neutral approach for a given set of stock views.

Table 9.1: Market neutral investing outcomes

Scenario 1: ABC share price rises, XYZ remains the same

After one year, shares in ABC rise to $3.00 and shares in XYZ close the year at $4.00.

Under this scenario, a profit of $1,000 will have accrued on the sale of the ABC shares and interest on the deposit of $4,000 would have also been added to the return. The total return is greater than simply buying the ABC shares outright.

Scenario 2: ABC rises, XYZ falls

After one year, shares in ABC rise to $3.00 and shares in XYZ close the year at $3.00.

Under this scenario, a profit of $1,000 will have accrued on the sale of the ABC shares. Shares in XYZ were sold at $4.00 and at the end of the year bought back at the prevailing market rate of $3.00. Another $1,000 profit is therefore made on the short sale. Interest on the deposit of $4,000 would have also been added to the return. The total return is again greater than simply buying the ABC shares outright.

Scenario 3: both ABC and XYZ rise

After one year, shares in ABC rise to $3.50 and shares in XYZ close the year at $5.00.

Under this scenario, a profit of $1,500 will have accrued on the sale of the ABC shares. Shares in XYZ were sold at $4.00 and at the end of the year bought back at the higher prevailing market rate of $5.00. Because the XYZ shares were sold at a low price and bought at a high price, a $1,000 loss has accrued on the short sale. Interest on the deposit of $4,000 would have also been added to the return. The total return is the profit of $1,500 on ABC less the loss on the short sale of XYZ of $1,000 plus the interest on the deposit. The result is a return that beats bank interest.

Scenario 4: both ABC and XYZ fall

After one year, shares in ABC fall to $2.00 and shares in XYZ close the year at $2.50.

Under this scenario, a profit of $1,500 will have accrued on the short sale of the XYZ shares. Shares in XYZ were sold at $4.00 and at the end of the year bought back at the lower prevailing market rate of $2.50. A loss of $1,000 is incurred on ABC. Interest on the deposit of $4,000 would have also been added to the return. The total return is the profit on XYZ of $1,500, less the loss on ABC of $1,000 plus the interest on the proceeds of the short sale. The return exceeds that available on interest-bearing securities.

Flexibility of market neutral strategies

It is relatively easy to demonstrate the key differences between market neutral and traditional investing and, in particular, the flexibility of the market neutral approach. Assume an equity analyst is following several stocks in a market and regards four of those seven stocks as mispriced (stocks A and F are undervalued, stocks E and G are overvalued).

The analyst's forecasts are as follows:

- Stock A: outperform

- Stock B: neutral

- Stock C: neutral

- Stock D: neutral

- Stock E: underperform

- Stock F: outperform

- Stock G: underperform.

In traditional 'long only' portfolios, active management is based on overweighting and underweighting stocks relative to a benchmark portfolio (usually an index such as the S&P/ ASX 200). In the first example, assume that the benchmark is equally weighted in stocks A through E — large banks, but excludes stocks F and G — smaller telcos. If the 'long only' manager starts by holding the benchmark portfolio and then wants to implement the analyst's views, he or she can overweight Stock A, add Stock F to the portfolio and sell as much of Stock E as they hold (which would be 20 per cent in this case). Unfortunately, they can't do anything about Stock G as this wasn't part of the benchmark. This is illustrated in Table 9.2, below.

Table 9.2: Long-only portfolio weightings

Stock	Benchmark weight	Portfolio weight	Over/under weight
A	20%	30%	+10%
B	20%	20%	
C	20%	20%	
D	20%	20%	
E	20%	0%	-20%
F	0%	10%	+10%
G	0%	0%	
Total	100%	100%	0%

The net result for the traditional long only portfolio is that stocks A and F are overweight by 10 per cent each, whereas stock E is underweight by 20 per cent. Stocks A and F make a long side and stock E makes the short side of the portfolio, which is effectively the active component of the long only portfolio for a traditional manager. The manager's portfolio comprises 40 per cent (20 per cent short and 20 per cent long) active exposure. Traditional managers tend to perform in line with the benchmark with a little room for outperformance by such overweighting and underweighting activities.

For the market neutral portfolio, 'shorts' aren't limited to the stocks held in the benchmark. Traditional managers are limited to selling stocks they already hold and therefore becoming 'underweight' in those holdings. This limitation does not exist for the market neutral manager. In addition, underperforming stocks that do appear in the benchmark can be sold beyond the benchmark weighting. Table 9.3, below, demonstrates a market neutral strategy based on the same stock views as above.

Table 9.3: Long-short market neutral portfolio weightings

Stock	Long side	Short side	Relative long–short
A	+25%	0%	
B	0%	0%	
C	0%	0%	
D	0%	0%	
E	0%	-25%	(F2) -25%
F	+25%	0%	
G	0%	-25%	(F1) -25%
Total	50%	50%	(F3) 0%

In the case of a market neutral strategy, there are some additional flexibilities (shown as F1, F2 and F3 in the table) that can be exploited.

First, the short side portfolio includes stock G, a stock outside the benchmark portfolio (F1).

Secondly, the weights of the short side portfolio are fully flexible, so the 'short position' in Stock E can be more than the 20 per cent benchmark weighting (F2).

In the case of the market neutral strategy the proportion that is actively invested is also fully flexible (F3). In this example, 'long positions' happen to be 50 per cent and 'short positions' also 50 per cent, but there is no reason why long positions could not be 150 per cent and shorts 150 per cent. Traditional portfolios are limited to longs of 100 per cent and shorts of 100 per cent. (In the special case where the traditional manager wants to buy only stocks outside the benchmark — if they held 100 per cent stocks outside the benchmark they would effectively be holding 100 per cent short positions in that benchmark!)

A market neutral strategy takes long and short positions in such a way that the impact of the overall market is minimised. Market neutral can imply dollar neutral. A dollar neutral strategy has zero net investment — that is, equal dollar amounts in long and short positions. Market neutral can also be beta neutral. A beta neutral strategy targets a zero total portfolio beta — that is, the beta of the long side equals the beta of the short side. Or it can be both dollar neutral and beta neutral.

The advantages of a market neutral portfolio are flexibility to:

- short assets outside the benchmark
- freely select weights of the short portfolio
- choose the level of active exposure (leverage)
- select the strategic benchmark.

These positive factors, however, are offset by:

- high transaction and stock borrowing costs
- short side liquidity costs
- theoretically unlimited downside risk (even though for practical purposes this risk is negligible in a well-diversified portfolio)
- high set-up and running costs resulting in higher management fees than with long-only funds.

Example — market neutral strategies

A market neutral portfolio is theoretically supposed to remove the market risk — that is, the directional risk of the market. In practice, however, there are always some uncovered risks, including stock selection risk, trade execution risk and market risk of unhedged positions. In addition, hedge positions may not completely eliminate market or sector risk. Therefore, active management is required to adjust positions regularly and keep the portfolio in line with acceptable market exposure.

There are many ways to implement a market neutral portfolio but almost all are impossible for the private investor, and this is one area where it is best left to a professional if some exposure is required.

Nevertheless, here we outline a strategy provided by Nawed Usmani, a US investment consultant with NRM capital. This strategy outlines an attempt not to eliminate market risk but to minimise it by keeping a low value of market exposure.

The strategy:

- Select stocks based on anticipated price performance relative to the other stocks of same sector — that is, select the leaders and laggards. Choose the leaders and laggards using the growth tools or value tools that we described earlier. Stick to large-cap stocks with high trading volume.

- Isolate the best expected performer and the worst expected performer. For example, isolate stocks with accelerating growth with reasonable P/E or growth with low P/E for a long position. Choose stocks with slower growth than their competitors or negative growth with high valuation for a short position.

- Buy shares in the leaders, which are anticipated to beat the market, and sell short shares in the laggards, which are expected to lag behind.

- When a sector is in an uptrend, portfolio holdings will be biased towards long positions. Consequently, in the downtrend, portfolio holdings will be biased towards short positions. The timing of initiating your long and short positions may vary based on sector trendlines. Therefore, at times there may not be any hedge for a particular position in portfolio.

- Portfolio may sell covered options on any long or short position when total annualised return (option premium plus profit in stock, if called or put) results in at least 30 per cent or better.

- All short positions in stocks, if not hedged, will carry a stop-loss order at all times. Initial stop-loss order will be placed between a 5 and 15 per cent loss level based on stock volatility and technical indicators.

Stop-loss order
A stop-loss order is an order to a stockbroker to sell a security when it reaches a particular value.

Once a month:

- Measure portfolio risk to ensure that sector holdings and overall portfolio conforms to market neutral investment style. The goal is to keep sector and market risk of the portfolio below standard deviation of comparable indices as much as possible. Appropriate adjustment may be made to align portfolio with the style.

- Adjust portfolio to ensure that all holdings are still meeting portfolio allocation and diversification guidelines.

- Review all stop-loss orders and adjust to protect profits or to reduce losses according to prevailing technical indicators and market conditions.

- Close and replace a position when there is an adverse change in company fundamentals.

The funds allocated for a position remain allocated for that position as long as the fundamentals are intact. The proceeds generated by the filling of a stop-loss order or temporary exit because of technical reasons can be transferred to money market funds until a replacement security is found.

Since one style of equity investing has not consistently outperformed another, a style-neutral approach can reduce total portfolio volatility. It eliminates the virtually impossible task of trying to estimate which style of equity investing will be in favour at a given point in time.

Simply put, market neutral funds aim to deliver above-market returns with lower risk by hedging bullish stock picks with an equivalent, but diversified, number of bearish, or short, bets. Investing in the market through such a strategy should result in an investment portfolio not correlated to overall market movements and insulated from systemic market risk.

For more information on market neutral investing and short selling, ask your stockbroker or other adviser, or see the ASX website (www.asx.com.au).

Your investment strategy

10

In this chapter, we will set out in simple point form the basic mechanics of six stock selection strategies that you might use in constructing your investing account portfolio. The objective is for you to revisit the material presented in the previous chapters and to formulate your own ideas regarding what strategy or strategies might suit you.

Most investment strategies employed by professional and private investors today were originally developed and tested by a handful of money managers, mainly in the US and the UK markets. Individually, these managers have become known as the 'gurus' of the investment markets and shelves full of books are dedicated to revealing their secrets. We would recommend that you take the time to read some of these books. In the meantime, to give you a taste of what you might discover, this chapter gives a brief overview of the investment philosophies of six such gurus.

The following stock selection ideas by no means represent the best or even an exhaustive collection. There are as many strategies as there are shares to invest in — and probably even more. The following techniques are simple models investors can investigate as a starting point to determine not only their effectiveness but also their suitability.

Before you conduct any investment activity you should speak with your financial adviser and determine the approach's suitability for you given your needs and circumstances.

Strategy #1: Upside potential

Once you have established a universe of shares to be considered, you can rank them in terms of their 'forecast' upside potential based on the current EPS and forecast EPS growth rate.

The mechanics

Obtain the following for your target company:

- share price
- EPS
- EPS growth rate.

Subjectively determine a growth hurdle (GH) — for example, 15 per cent. Calculate a forecast share price by multiplying the EPS by the EPS growth rate. Now determine the rate of growth required to attain the forecast price. Finally rank your universe by this rate to find those companies that are showing the greatest promise based on what the analysts believe the companies respective future earnings and expected growth rates are.

In Table 10.1, opposite, we look at two companies — company A and company B. The shares of both companies are trading at $1.10 and both are expected to earn 10 cents per share next year. This puts the shares for both companies on a prospective P/E ratio of 11 times next year's earnings. The two companies differ, however, when the rate of earnings growth is compared. Company A is expected to see earnings grow by 25 per cent to earn 10 cents per share next year while company B is expected to see 15 per cent growth in earnings. Using the formula we described above (multiplying the growth rate by the forecast earnings per share) we find that company A may have greater upside potential.

Table 10.1: Calculating the potential upside

	Company A	Company B
Current price	$1.10	$1.10
Forecast EPS	$0.10	$0.10
EPS Growth rate	25%	15%
Forecast price	$2.50	$1.50
Potential upside	127.27%	36.36%

Importantly, the formula we have used contains no hidden secrets to make it work. The resulting 'forecast' price is simply that — a forecast. There is no requirement for the shares to go to this price so the forecast may indeed prove to be incorrect. What we are doing here, however, is ranking the shares in descending order, with those that have the greatest 'forecast' potential at the top, down to those that have the least upside potential or even a measured downside risk.

As we have already mentioned, before these techniques are adopted, a universe of shares must first be established. The above method then serves to rank those companies in order of your chosen merit system. Beyond this point, further research can be conducted into those companies that rank highly — say, the top 10 to 15 stocks, or the top 10 to 20, could form the first portfolio. Remember to crosscheck your selections with an adviser to determine a particular stock's suitability for your goals.

Strategy #2: Projected price range

This model is a variation on the above theme. It is simpler and will make more sense when you explain it to others such as your broker if you are utilising the services of a full-service adviser.

The mechanics

Select your investment universe — usually 50 to 100 companies. Establish the historical five-year P/E range for each share. (Or use any number of years you prefer, the more the better.) Calculate the average P/E for each by adding the five-year P/E high and the five-year P/E low then dividing the total by two. Establish next year's forecast EPS. Multiply next year's forecast EPS by the average P/E to come up with next year's price target. Now rank the universe with those currently trading the furthest below the forecast price target at the top of the list. The 10 to 20 shares at the top of the list may represent the most undervalued (relatively speaking) given their historical P/E ranges.

Let's look at an example to see the technique in operation. Imagine that shares in company A have traded at a P/E high of 17.75 times earnings and a P/E low of 6.69 times. The average P/E for company A has therefore been 12.2 — (17.75 + 6.69) ÷ 2. The anticipated earnings per share for the coming year is 30 to 38 cents per share. After multiplying this by the average P/E of 12.2 times, we obtain a 'projected' price range for the shares of between $3.66 and $4.63. If shares are trading within this range, this method suggests there is still some potential for the shares to rise. However, what we are ideally looking for is both the lower and upper bands of next year's forecast price range to be well above the current trading price.

It then becomes a relatively simple matter of ranking companies by the greatest price gap between the current trading price and the lower end of the band.

Strategy #3: A longer term approach

The next strategy picks shares based on a longer term investment time frame, using growth potential based on return on equity, debt to equity and dividend yield.

The mechanics

Select the investment universe. Select the top 25 by return on equity. Remove any company that has made a loss in the last 10 years. From the remaining companies rank by debt to equity from lowest to highest debt to equity ratios. Remove the bottom half with the highest ratios. Now rank the remaining companies by dividend yield in descending order. The issues at the top may represent the most out of favour, and so undervalued (relatively speaking), given the higher dividend yield.

Strategy #4: A medium-term approach

The fourth strategy picks shares based on a medium-term investment time frame using P/E ratios.

The mechanics

Take the top 100 industrial companies by market capitalisation. Rank them by P/E ratio in ascending order (lowest to highest). Isolate the top 30 (those 30 with the lowest P/Es). Own those securities with underlying businesses that have the following characteristics:

- current assets at least 1.5 times current liabilities
- debt less than 110 per cent of current assets
- no losses in the last five years
- a stable dividend record
- earnings this year higher than last year
- price less than 1.2 times net tangible assets.

Re-rank and re-weight at the end of 12 (or 24) months and repeat the process.

Strategy #5: A longer term approach using dividend yield

This strategy is again based on a long-term approach. The method for picking shares in this strategy is based on dividend yields.

The mechanics

Take the top 100 industrial companies by market capitalisation. Rank them by dividend yield from highest to lowest. Take the top 10 stocks. Hold for 12 months. Re-rank and re-weight at the end of twelve months and repeat the process.

Strategy #6: A longer term approach using price/sales ratios

The final strategy is also based on a long-term time frame, this time using price/sales ratios.

The mechanics

Isolate the top 100 companies by market capitalisation. Rank them by price/sales per share. Isolate those with a price/sales ratio of less than one. From this list, select the 10 companies with shares that have risen the most in the previous twelve months. Allocate equal dollar amounts to the 10 and then review and re-weight in twelve months time.

Getting the picture? Ranking companies by their respective internal strengths and weaknesses, by the valuations imposed on their shares by the market, or by a combination of the two, are all valid methods of stock selection for the purposes of portfolio construction.

Some of the strategies above were originally postulated by Benjamin Graham. The final strategy looks for companies that are still cheap but have had a good run in the market over the previous year. It recognises the idea that 'the trend is your friend' and that the strength in the stock may be for reasons not widely known or understood in the market. This strategy is taking advantage of that market 'inefficiency'.

The above strategies are as simple as they all appear to be. They have all been tested and the dogged adherence to strategies like these has seen individual years of stellar outperformance. (And, as with any method, they have seen individual years of underperformance.) While the past has been kind to these strategies, there is no guarantee that any will work in the future. The important message here is that you must develop a strategy of some description and, even more importantly, once it is developed, you must apply it consistently.

Investment gurus

Before we move on from strategies for long-term investing, we will consider some of the world's best money managers and their techniques.

Peter Lynch

From 1977 to 1990, Peter Lynch steered the Fidelity Fund to a total return of 2,510 per cent, or five times the 500 per cent return of the S&P 500 index. In his first book *One up on Wall Street*, Peter Lynch described a variety of strategies that individual investors can use to duplicate his success. These strategies divide attractive stocks into different categories, each characterised by different criteria. Among those most easy to identify using quantitative research are fast growers, slow growers and stalwarts, with special criteria applied to cyclical and financial stocks. Lynch's individual categories and criteria are outlined below.

Fast growers

According to Peter Lynch, the characteristics of fast-growing companies are:

- they have little or no debt
- their earnings growth is 20 to 50 per cent a year
- their P/E ratio is below the company's earnings growth rate, meaning the PE/G ratio is less than one.

This approach is an exciting method because it combines growth with value. Using the above criteria seeks out those companies that show strong growth but are trading at the lowest prices relative to their earnings growth rates.

Slow growers

The characteristics of slow-growing companies are:

- they are in the top quartile of sales revenue
- they have high dividend payout ratios

- they have sales that are growing faster than inventories

- they have a low yield-adjusted PE/G ratio.

Peter Lynch argues you should invest in these companies for their premium income. They are often ignored during boom times but investors will come flooding back when the first sign of a downturn is sniffed.

Stalwarts

The characteristics of stalwarts are:

- they have recorded positive earnings every year for the last five years

- they have a debt to equity ratio of 0.33 or less

- their sales growth rates are increasing in line with, or ahead of, inventories

- they have a low yield-adjusted PE/G ratio.

Generally, stalwarts have only moderate earnings growth but can have a potential for significant share price gains over the medium term if they can be purchased at attractive prices.

William O'Neil

William O'Neil become popular in 1984 when he launched *Investor's Daily*, a national business newspaper in the United States. Regarded as a growth and momentum investor, O'Neil pioneered data mining by computer. By studying the characteristics of the best 500 growth companies over the last 30 years, he developed a rigorous stock selection discipline based on numerous fundamental and technical factors.

Common characteristics of O'Neil's target companies are as follows:

- they are industry-leaders

- they have a strong relative strength readings (indicating that they have performed very well relative to the overall market)

- they have recorded a perfect earnings record of substantial EPS increases over time

- they are poised to reach new highs following at least eight weeks of consolidation (trading within a range, while showing no definitive trend either up or down).

O'Neil's strategy is extremely aggressive and only appropriate for investors who are comfortable paying a premium for fast-growing companies. This is momentum investing in its purest form and harbours all of its dangers.

David Dreman

David Dreman's contrarian investment style suits those who like to go against the consensus opinion of the time. Dreman is manager of the Kemper-Dreman High-Return Equity Fund and an investment columnist for *Forbes* magazine. From 1990 to 1997, Dreman's fund outpaced the S&P 500 by an average of 3.6 percentage points per year.

Stocks must generally be in large companies and must be out of favour due to public apathy, delirium or naiveté. They must also meet the following criteria under Dreman's plan:

- good earnings growth

- good return on equity

- low debt-to-equity ratio.

Martin Zweig

Martin Zweig is a growth investor and a renowned newsletter writer. Zweig searches for stocks that meet a long host of earnings criteria including:

- quarterly earnings that are positive and growing faster than they were:

  - a year ago

  - in the preceding three quarters

  - over the preceding three years

- annual earnings that are up for at least the past five years

- sales that are growing as fast as or faster than earnings, since cost-cutting and other non-revenue-producing measures alone can't support earnings growth forever

- a P/E ratio of at least five — to weed out weak companies — but no more than three times the current market P/E or 43, whichever is lower.

James P. O'Shaughnessy

James O'Shaughnessy forced many professional and amateur investors alike to rethink their investment beliefs when he published his 1996 bestseller, *What works on Wall Street*.

Based on his research, O'Shaughnessy developed two key investment strategies: 'cornerstone growth' and 'cornerstone value'.

The cornerstone growth strategy invests in companies with:

- a market capitalisation of at least $150 million

- a price-to-sales ratio below 1.5

- persistent earnings growth

- performance results that are among the market's best over the prior 12 months.

This strategy makes sense for value-oriented growth investors who have the patience and personality to stick with a purely quantitative investment approach.

The cornerstone value strategy, on the other hand, invests in large companies with:

- strong sales

- strong cash flows

- the highest dividend yields.

Benjamin Graham

In 1934, Graham co-authored a book entitled *Security analysis: principles and techniques* with colleague David Dodd. This book contained a lasting message — the rational investor does not play to market swings. Graham and Dodd described the market as a voting machine, not a weighing machine and insisted that the market was often illogical. In 1949, Graham followed his original work with a second book *The intelligent investor*. This book stressed the importance of developing a 'margin of safety'. Graham suggested that investors should look for large gaps between a stock's worth and its price. It was this work that attracted the attention of Warren Buffett, who first enrolled in Graham's class at Columbia in 1950 and then applied to work for Graham at his funds management firm between 1954 and 1956.

Graham relied heavily on a quantitative (numbers) approach to evaluate businesses. Using the balance sheet and a number of numerical tests, Graham often found companies priced below net asset value. Graham often looked for businesses that displayed the following characteristics:

- debt/equity less than 50 per cent
- price/book less than 1.2
- current ratio greater than 2
- quick ratio greater than 1
- price/net working capital less than 1.

Essentially, if a business's shares were worth $1 and were selling for 40 cents, Graham was interested. To be fair to modern-day investors, these criteria are very restrictive and you will find it difficult to find businesses that meet all of these criteria without following the markets every single day. Indeed the criteria were so restrictive they led to Buffett considering the arguments put forward by another successful investor, Charlie Munger, and formulating his own approach before teaming up with Munger at Berkshire

Hathaway. The general themes of Graham's theory, however, are still relevant to investors today.

Throughout Graham's life, there were 14 investment philosophies he consistently espoused. They are summarised below:

1   Be an investor, not a speculator. Don't try to profit from market movements.

2   Question whether the company is worth its market capitalisation.

3   Apply the Net Current Asset Value (NCAV) rule. Find NCAV by subtracting all of a firm's liabilities (including preferred shares) from current assets. Purchase shares that are below their NCAV per share level.

4   Determine the intrinsic value of a company's shares.

5   Regard corporate figures with suspicion. Be wary of manipulation of earnings through accounting changes.

6   Don't worry about precision. While you can never expect to be exact, an appropriate margin of safety should protect an investor.

7   Don't worry about the mathematics. You do not need maths beyond simple algebra.

8   Diversification rule #1: hold a minimum of 25 per cent in bonds and 25 per cent in common stocks.

9   Diversification rule #2: try to have at least 30 different holdings of equities.

10 When in doubt, stick to quality. Good earnings, solid dividend payout histories, low debt and reasonable P/Es are all signs of quality stocks.

11 Use dividends as a sign. Risky growth stocks seldom pay dividends. Look for companies who have treated their shareholders well and have a consistent and positive dividend policy.

12 Defend your shareholder rights. Complain if you feel
    management is not acting in shareholders' best
    interests.

13 Be patient. Be prepared financially and
    psychologically for poor results in the short term.

14 Think for yourself. Be independent and never stop
    thinking.

Managing your investing account

An investment portfolio can comprise a range of assets, not just shares. The share component itself can often be broken down further into the core, long-term investing account and the speculative account. In this chapter, we get down to some of the practicalities of managing your investing account, including:

■ selling shares

■ building and re-weighting your portfolio

■ moving current investments into your investing account.

The rationale and processes employed in each of these activities must be clearly defined as part of your investment strategy before you begin. For example, you must determine when and why you would potentially sell a stock before you even buy it. We examine the benefits of dollar cost averaging when it comes to building your portfolio and two methods of periodically re-weighting your portfolio to keep it in line with your strategy.

Selling

Before the technique for selecting shares has been developed, tested and implemented, a method for exiting also needs to be established.

Using purely fundamental analysis and a long-term approach for the investing account, there are only a few reasons why you should ever be tempted to sell.

Some typical (and logical) reasons for selling are:

- when the fundamentals no longer make the shares qualify
- when conditions or management change adversely
- when 'fair value' has been reached
- when better value has been found elsewhere.

Rational, unemotional approach to selling

The above reasons indicate that selling is always conducted in a rational, logical and unemotional way. Notice that the reasons 'sell when you fear a market decline' or 'sell when your friend tells you the stock is falling' do not appear in the above list. Notice also that the reason 'I have changed my mind' also does not appear as a justifiable reason for exiting. By doing the work earlier to select the shares that have met the criteria, there is little need to apply any emotion at all to the selling process.

If your strategy was simply to always own the top 15 companies by market capitalisation, when one of those companies dropped out of the top 15, in accordance with your strategy, it would need to be sold and replaced with the new fifteen largest company. Similarly, if the fundamental reasons you purchased the company for in the first place no longer exist, the shares can no longer be held. This is a valid reason for selling.

Alternatively, if the price rises so much that it represents fair value, you might also be justified in selling. But even then you may not because another calculation could discover there is further upside potential beyond what you originally forecast. You would not remove a star player from your sport's team simply because he or she became too good would you? So why sell a share simply because it is going up? Remember that Buffett might hold on 'forever' if the company continues to earn above average rates of return on equity, the management is honest and the market does not overprice the stock.

Indeed, another criterion for selling may be to only sell something if and when an opportunity that is clearly better comes along. Otherwise, you can hold onto what you have originally purchased.

Know when and why to sell *before* you buy

Whatever the reason you choose, the important thing is that the selling decision must be part of your original strategy. You must choose your reason to sell *before* you actually buy. An investor's confidence will increase and a strategy will be adhered to when the circumstances for triggering a sale are known well in advance of the actual event occurring.

Takeovers

There have been several studies conducted by universities in the United States that have suggested that takeovers are generally not positive for the shareholders of the acquiring company. While this is not true on every individual takeover, the results probably suggest that takeovers, particularly hostile ones, generally lead to inflated prices being paid that are difficult to achieve above average returns on. As a result, the returns from the entire new entity fall.

Building and re-weighting your portfolio

Once you have developed a strategy for selecting shares, including criteria for when you might sell them, the main question that remains before you can begin building your portfolio is the timing of your purchases. We will look at one method of dealing with that question here — that is, dollar cost averaging.

Dollar cost averaging

Dollar cost averaging is the process whereby a set amount is allocated to specific investments at regular intervals. It is intended to lower the average price paid for the investment.

Having selected and purchased the shares, your next job is to manage your portfolio. An important aspect of that is the regular review and re-weighting of the components of your portfolio in line with your investment objectives. We will look at a simple method of re-weighting a portfolio and then discuss why you might want to consider an alternative approach.

Adding to your portfolio using dollar cost averaging

Part of your planning may be to add to your investments over time, rather than merely let a single investment grow. The benefits of compounding are magnified by averaging the prices we purchase the selected securities at and this can certainly improve a strategy. Dollar cost averaging is a simple approach that has other inherent benefits. While there are other more aggressive methods that can accelerate gains (and losses) even faster, we will engage the dollar cost averaging approach here.

When is the best time to buy? The truth is that no-one knows for sure. When stocks go up, the best time is always 'yesterday', but when stocks fall, the best time is 'sometime in the future'. Dollar cost averaging is an effective means by which an investor is able to reduce the risk of poor timing. It has the effect of spreading the purchase over several months or years, thereby mitigating the risk of purchasing the entire investment at too high a price. While the advantages are obvious there are also risks. The risk is that the price of the chosen securities continues to rise and never drops back to the price at which the initial investment was made. In this case, it would have been better to make the entire investment at the beginning, rather than spread it out over time.

Dollar cost averaging works like this — you simply invest the exact same dollar amount into your security selections at regular ongoing intervals. For example, suppose the company Newmine Shipping was your target. Rather than purchase all the stock you are aiming to acquire at once, you spread your purchase out over six months or a year, buying equal dollar amounts — say, $1,000 — each time.

Dollar cost averaging for a single stock

To better illustrate the benefits and the costs of such a strategy, let's work with an example. We'll start by looking at buying just one company's shares and then move to a portfolio structure. Suppose you want to invest $50,000 in one company today, and the shares are trading at $10. You don't know if the shares will be trading at $20 or $5 at the end of the year. To mitigate the risk associated with making a poor timing decision, it is possible to spread the purchase out over twelve months, investing approximately $4,167 on the first business day of each month, regardless of where the shares are trading at that time.

To examine the impact of our decision let's look at three different events.

Say the shares start the year at $10 and finish at $21. Each month you invest $4,167. Table 11.1, below, shows the average share price paid over the year and the total number of shares bought.

Table 11.1: Dollar cost averaging in a rising market

Scenario 1 (one share) $50,000

Company/share price

Month	Share price	Invest	No. of Shares
January	$10	$4,167	416
February	11	$4,167	378
March	12	$4,167	347
April	13	$4,167	320
May	15	$4,167	277
June	19	$4,167	219
July	18	$4,167	231
August	17	$4,167	245
September	16	$4,167	260
October	17	$4,167	245
November	19	$4,167	219
December	21	$4,167	198
		$50,004	3,355
	Average Price	$14.90	

In the previous example, had you purchased $50,000 worth of shares over the course of the year, you would have purchased a total of 3,355 shares at an average price of $14.90. This may not seem particularly remarkable until it is pointed out that the shares actually traded higher than this price for 8 of the 12 months or two-thirds of the year. In this case, during only 4 of the 12 months were the shares cheaper than the average price achieved. In terms of probability, the investor had only a 33 per cent chance of buying the shares cheaper over the year.

Imagine, however, if the share price fell — say, from $10 to $7. In Table 11.2, below, the average share price paid over the year and the total number of shares bought in this situation is shown.

Table 11.2: Dollar cost averaging in a falling market

Scenario 2 (one share) $50,000

Company/share price

Month	Share price	Invest	No. of Shares
January	$10	$4,167	416
February	9	$4,167	463
March	8	$4,167	520
April	8	$4,167	520
May	9	$4,167	463
June	8	$4,167	520
July	8	$4,167	520
August	7	$4,167	595
September	5	$4,167	833
October	8	$4,167	520
November	4	$4,167	1,041
December	7	$4,167	595
		$50,004	7,006
	Average Price	$7.14	

Source: Investors Advantage. Reproduced with permission.

In the above example, using dollar cost averaging to invest $50,000, you would have bought 7,006 shares for an average price of $7.14. Again, this doesn't seem particularly amazing until you observe that the shares traded higher than this level for eight months of the year. Further, despite the fact that shares were purchased earlier in the year at $10, $9 and $8, the average entry price is only 6 cents away from the current price. The price only needs to rise 14 cents, or 2 per cent, for the breakeven point on this investment to be reached. This is a far cry from the alternative. Had you invested the entire $50,000 into the share at the start of the year, you would now be down 30 per cent and you would require a 43 per cent gain in the share price to break even.

Finally, imagine the share price falls and then rises back to the original entry price. Table 11.3, below, again shows the average share price paid over a year and the total number of shares bought in this situation.

Table 11.3: Dollar cost averaging in a volatile market

Scenario 3 (one share) $50,000

Company/share price

Month	Share price	Invest	No. of Shares
January	$10	$4,167	416
February	7	$4,167	595
March	6	$4,167	694
April	5	$4,167	833
May	4	$4,167	1,041
June	6	$4,167	694
July	7	$4,167	595
August	6	$4,167	694
September	5	$4,167	833
October	8	$4,167	520
November	9	$4,167	463
December	10	$4,167	416
		$50,004	7,794
	Average Price	$6.42	

In the above example, using dollar cost averaging to invest $50,000, you would have bought 7,794 shares for an average price of $6.42. Despite the fact that the shares are at the same price at the end of the year as they were at the beginning, you have made a profit of 55 per cent! This example highlights the biggest benefit of dollar cost averaging. When you are investing constant dollar amounts, you can buy more shares at potentially cheaper prices. This lowers the average price and means that the price does not need to rise as far before profits accrue.

Dollar cost averaging for your entire portfolio

Now we'll look at initiating a dollar cost averaging approach to an entire portfolio. Suppose you have $60,000 to invest in five companies ($12,000 per company). Rather than invest all of it today, another approach is to spread the investment out over a year, making twelve instalments of $1,000 in each company.

Table 11.4, below, shows the course of share prices for the five companies throughout the year. Notice that three stocks are lower at the end of the year and two are higher.

Table 11.4: Prices for five stocks over a year

Month	Company 1	Company 2	Company 3	Company 4	Company 5
January	$11.00	$7.00	$8.00	$15.00	$11.00
February	$11.00	$8.00	$9.00	$13.00	$9.00
March	$12.00	$9.00	$8.00	$14.00	$6.00
April	$13.00	$7.00	$8.00	$13.00	$5.00
May	$15.00	$6.00	$9.00	$12.00	$4.00
June	$19.00	$5.00	$8.00	$11.00	$6.00
July	$18.00	$7.00	$8.00	$13.00	$7.00
August	$17.00	$8.00	$7.00	$14.00	$6.00
September	$16.00	$9.00	$5.00	$16.00	$5.00
October	$15.00	$10.00	$8.00	$19.00	$8.00
November	$11.00	$11.00	$4.00	$18.00	$9.00
December	$9.00	$11.00	$7.00	$16.00	$10.00

Table 11.5, opposite, now illustrates the numbers of shares in each of the five companies that were purchased each month using the dollar cost averaging approach. The totals at the bottom of each column reveal the final number of shares that were purchased by the end of the year.

While we know that looking at these numbers is very uninteresting, if you do the sums on what the portfolio is worth at the end of the year, you will probably be surprised. If you had invested $60,000 by buying $1,000 worth of each of the five companies throughout the year, your portfolio would be worth $69,033 at the end of the year.

That's a first year return on the invested funds of 15 per cent. Had you invested all of the $60,000 at the prices available in January, the portfolio would be worth around $62,884 — a return of 4.8 per cent. Admittedly, a 4.8 per cent return when three of your shares have fallen is not disastrous, but by spreading the purchases over the year, you have beaten it more than three times over.

Table 11.5: Numbers of shares purchased each month

Month	Company 1	Company 2	Company 3	Company 4	Company 5
January	91	143	125	67	91
February	91	125	111	77	111
March	83	111	125	71	167
April	77	143	125	77	200
May	67	167	111	83	250
June	53	200	125	91	167
July	56	143	125	77	143
August	59	125	143	71	167
September	63	111	200	63	200
October	67	100	125	53	125
November	91	91	250	56	111
December	111	91	143	63	100
	907	1,549	1,708	848	1,831

Including brokerage in the calculations

Most experienced investors will complain that we haven't included brokerage in the calculations and that brokerage is much higher in the dollar cost averaging approach rather than the purchasing all the shares at once. The response to this misconception has two parts. Firstly, there is a good possibility that a full-service broker will negotiate a better deal if he or she knows in advance what you are intending to do over the course of the next few years. Secondly, transaction costs should not prevent you from generating extra percentage point returns.

We illustrate this second point using a brokerage rate of $30 per trade. Buying all the shares at the start of the year and spreading the $60,000 evenly over the five companies, giving a total of five trades, would give a portfolio value at the end of the year of $62,727 — or a return of 4.5 per cent after brokerage costs.

The dollar cost averaging approach results in a total of 60 trades with a $30 charge on every trade. Purchasing the shares this way results in a portfolio value of $66,674 or a 11.1 per cent return. As previously stated, don't let small differences in transaction charges stop you from generating a better return.

Re-weighting your portfolio

Selecting shares and purchasing them are important parts of applied portfolio management. But 'managing' a portfolio should involve more than simply buying and holding. Here we explore one method of re-weighting — another important aspect of portfolio management.

Re-weighting is the process by which you will effectively review your investments and make adjustments. Like every other step in the process, this must also be part of your strategy and adhered to rigorously. It must be clearly defined, have an answer for every contingency and be simple to follow.

The first step is to define a time frame for review. It may be annually or semi-annually but we would suggest no more frequently. Remember that the investing account is generally for your long-term investment portfolio and, while reviews are essential, too frequent reviews will defeat the purpose and indeed tempt you to stray from the course you have set yourself.

Equal re-weighting of a portfolio

Suppose in the first year your selected strategy picked the securities outlined below. In each security you invested $12,000 over the course of the year following the dollar cost averaging approach we outlined earlier.

At the end of the first year the individual values were as shown in Table 11.6, opposite.

Table 11.6: Portfolio values after one year

	Start Year 1	End Year 1
Company 1	$12,000	$8,162
Company 2	$12,000	$17,042
Company 3	$12,000	$11,956
Company 4	$12,000	$13,564
Company 5	$12,000	$18,310
	$60,000	**$69,034**

As the shares that are in your portfolio have been bought based on the reasons outlined in your strategy rather than market sentiment, one method of review is to acknowledge that the economic conditions that made one company do well over the year may not continue. Conversely, the economic drivers that caused another security to perform poorly throughout the year may also be about to change. With this in mind it might make sense to reduce the holdings of the company that has done well and add to the investment that has not performed as well. The reasoning behind this process is that when economic conditions change, we have added more shares to the portfolio of the company that has underperformed, which could result in significant returns when future gains are compounded by the additional shares held.

Re-weighting is initially a simple matter of calculating the value of the portfolio at the end of the year, and dividing the total by the number of companies held in the portfolio (in this case five). The number produced becomes the weight that each company in the portfolio should have. In the above example, you would need to hold $13,806.70 worth of each company's shares for the following year. This amount we'll call the 're-weighted amount'.

Because some company's shares have risen in value beyond this re-weighted amount, it might be appropriate to sell the overweight securities. Investors could then elect to put the proceeds from the sales towards purchasing more shares in the companies the share price of which had fallen by the end of the year, resulting in a lower balance than the re-weighted amount.

Table 11.7, below, shows how the portfolio would be reweighted.

Table 11.7: Re-weighting your portfolio

	Start Year 1	End Year 1	Adjustments	Start Year 2
Company 1	$12,000	$8,162	$5,644	$13,806.70
Company 2	$12,000	$17,042	-$3,235	$13,806.70
Company 3	$12,000	$11,956	$1,851	$13,806.70
Company 4	$12,000	$13,564	$243	$13,806.70
Company 5	$12,000	$18,310	-$4,503	$13,806.70
	$60,000	$69,034	$0	$69,034

Let's follow the process through with company 1.

At the beginning of the first year you invested $12,000 in company 1. By the end of the year that investment had fallen to $8,162. As outlined, the re-weighted amount for each company stands at $13,807. Therefore, $5,644 will have to be spent purchasing additional shares in company 1.

At first, adding to a poor performing share may not appear wise. However, if we assume that you have done the research in the first place, and the company met your stock selection criteria at the beginning and still does at the end of the first year, adding to the number of shares held could compound the benefits of the dollar cost averaging process even further (if you had used this strategy) when the share rises.

The money to purchase additional shares comes from the proceeds of the sales of the shares that have risen to a value beyond the calculated re-weighted amount. In the previous example the proceeds come from the sale of $3,235 worth of company 2 shares and $4,503 worth of company 5 shares.

By equally re-weighting, as illustrated above, we are giving each security an equal chance of responding to their individual performance drivers. We prevent ourselves from being overweight or underweight in any stock.

The final benefit is that the process can assist in *selling high and buying low*.

An alternative method of re-weighting

The above strategy may seem logical but it is by no means the only way to re-weight or review a portfolio. Indeed, some portfolio managers argue the exact opposite — for an extremely long-term approach, selling something that is doing well is most likely to be counter-intuitive. Why sell your best performing stock? So there are alternative methods.

One such method is to remove the non-performing securities and replace them with stocks that have characteristics that today resemble those in your portfolio that are doing well. This method, over time, creates a new benchmark — your portfolio itself.

Each time a new security is added to replace one which is being removed (if there are any), the new security must display more impressive characteristics than the characteristics displayed by the current securities you are holding. The benchmark is therefore constantly being raised with the goal being a strong performing portfolio to be held for an extremely long time. If no more impressive securities can be found, no re-weighting takes place, but the review has been completed.

Moving current investments into your investing account

We have now almost completed the task of designing, building and readjusting the investing account but what about the situation where you already have an existing investment in shares that don't meet your new criteria?

There are several choices. The first is that you sell everything and start again. However, we would not suggest this course — it is neither tax-effective nor intelligent. Such a recommendation without review is a careless one.

Another alternative is a significant improvement — hold everything and wait until the holdings meet the criteria for your new stock selection process. When they do meet the criteria, enter them into the portfolio. This is a little better as the tax impact of selling may be deferred indefinitely. The problem, however, is twofold. Firstly, there may be holdings that will never meet the criteria for the investing account. Provided they no longer meet the reasons you purchased them in the first place, or you cannot remember why you purchased them, or it is not a company the shares of which you purchased 15 years ago that now provide a dividend yield of 50 per cent, selling may be acceptable. Secondly, while you wait, you could be missing more impressive gains by not investing in a more defined and disciplined approach.

The final method is a little more involved. Start the disciplined strategic approach immediately. Don't miss out on the benefits we outlined at the beginning of the book. Start small if need be and simultaneously review the existing holdings. Over time, the relative size of the old holdings will fall as the value of any contribution of the new approach rises. Any shares that no longer measure up to your criteria for purchasing them in the first place should be removed or, if they are speculative, added to the speculating account. Continue to hold any shares that you are happy owning, provided the reasoning is logical and rational rather than emotional.

A final word on the investing account

The process of learning never ends. Your strategy will evolve over time and mistakes will be made. Let them happen but learn from them — as Lord Byron said, 'We learn more from mistakes than from confusion'.

Don't fret over the mistakes. By diversifying appropriately, the adverse impact from the mistakes should be small and can quickly be recovered if you have learnt from the errors. If you have sufficient funds, it is possible to diversify across shares and then across strategies as well to further mitigate the adverse impact of any one mistake.

The investing account is generally for the long term and as such filling it will take time. Don't be tempted to rush the process. As Warren Buffett points out, the right inputs should provide positive results over the long term. Indeed, Buffett's following quote, from a Berkshire Hathaway annual conference, is apt for wrapping up our examination of the investing account:

Should you choose, however, to construct your portfolio, there are a few thoughts worth remembering. Intelligent investing is not complex, though that is far from saying that it is easy. What an investor needs is the ability to correctly evaluate selected businesses. Note that word 'selected'. You don't have to be an expert on every company, or even many. You only have to be able to evaluate companies within your circle of competence. The size of that circle is not very important; knowing its boundaries, however, is vital.

Your speculating account

We now move onto topics relating to trading on your speculating account, including:

- how to feed your speculating account
- trading objectives and elements of success
- mechanical approaches to trading.

Your approach to speculating, if you do decide to speculate, should be quite different from that taken for your long-term investments, as the objectives of each are quite different. First of all, we suggest you only consider speculating with some portion of excess gains from your investing account, and then only with money you can afford to lose.

While you may be attracted to the excitement of speculating, your real objective should be to maximise risk-adjusted returns. That is, you should recognise that you will have some losing trades and implement filters to reduce their number. You then need to make sure you cut short any losses that do occur and let your profits run.

Rather than the extensive use of fundamental analysis, we recommend a mechanical approach to speculating — that is, one that can be quantified and its success measured. A mechanical trading system involves clearly defined rules regarding when and what to buy and sell, what risks to take and when to stop trading.

Your speculating account

For many investors it is not necessary to speculate and for others it is not desirable. The choice to avoid speculation is as valid as choosing to participate.

The speculating account consists of speculative investments. Large short-term gains are expected here and while there are no guarantees that you will make money, there are some techniques that have provided curiously robust historical results. Of course, you don't have to speculate if you don't want to and because of the way you will be allocating funds, you don't need to speculate to become wealthier through the stockmarket. If you consider yourself relatively conservative or you are afraid of losing money — any money — don't speculate. It is entirely possible that you will improve your financial position just with the investing account.

If, however, you do want to speculate, you will need to set up at least two accounts. One account will need to be dedicated to speculative purposes and in the coming pages we will explain some of the techniques that successful speculators use in an attempt to profit from price volatility.

Importantly, many of the principles we discussed in regards to the investing account have absolutely no place here. In the investing account we addressed diversification and the use of fundamental stock selection models. In the speculating account, however, the focus is not diversification but concentration. Here, our objective is not slow and steady gains. Rather our goal is a large short-term return. Because of the way we will structure our funds, any loss should not be a major concern. A loss in the speculating account is certainly not going to have an adverse impact on our long-term financial goals.

How to fund your speculating account

For many investors new to the stockmarket, the lure of speculation is mouth watering. Indeed, the promise of riches beyond imagining are perpetuated by the stories we hear of individuals buying a stock at 10 cents and riding it all the way to $20 and retiring at age 30. For every story like that, however, there are a thousand investors for whom such an event remains just a dream. Unfortunately, many of these people will continue to try, all the while forgetting to build an investing account. When these investors reach the end of their road, they often realise they have failed to set aside anything of value. All their energy went into speculating and now that it has failed, there is very little wealth created and there is very little time left to do so.

To avoid this situation, it is generally beneficial to focus on the investing account now and then speculate later. This is the approach we will explore for the purposes of funding the speculating account.

Excess gains from investing used to fund speculating account and vice versa

To fund the speculating account, you can set yourself an excess return level on the investing account. The investing account will operate as the feeder for the speculating account. The speculating account can also feed into the investing account. Excess gains in the investing account can allow a little speculating and any excess gains from speculating can go back into the investing account.

On the speculating ledger, the wins are generally outnumbered by the losses so invest the proceeds wisely — back into the investing account. For example, suppose you set yourself a target for the investing account of 15 per cent per year. That is, you would like to double your money every five years. Of course, setting the target does not mean you will achieve it. However, in some years you will and in others you may even exceed it. It is in those years — the ones where you exceed your desired rate of return — that it may be possible to extract some funds for speculating.

For example, if you achieved a 21 per cent return in a particular year and your target was 15 per cent, there would be 6 per cent in excess gains. Some of these excess returns can be used for speculation. The years of a 21 per cent gain on your investment account are too few and far between and too important to eschew compounding over the long term — remembering that only funds you are prepared to lose should be moved into your speculating account. Somewhere in the vicinity of a quarter of these excess returns — that is, around 1.5 per cent of the original investment, in this example — should be used for speculating by most small investors.

So for an investor who starts with $100,000 and achieves a 21 per cent return, or $21,000 profit before tax, there exists a potential $1,500 of excess returns that can be put to the task of speculating.

An investor with $250,000 in the investing account who achieves a 21 per cent return can expect to have $302,000 in the investing account at the end of the year. Of the 21 per cent or $52,500 profit, the investor may choose to use $3,750 to speculate.

Too conservative?

Initially this may not seem like much and admittedly it does appear to be conservative but if you raise the amount remember — the risks in speculating are significant and many of those risks cannot be mitigated at all. Those with more experience in speculating might devote a higher percentage to the task. The fact remains that too high a percentage could be *hazardous to your wealth*. For anyone with little or no experience in speculating, the smaller the allocation to begin with the better, as a high proportion of speculators lose money.

Regardless of how much you put into the speculating account, you must act in a professional manner and apply all of the discipline required to trade effectively.

Don't trade with money you can't afford to lose

Anecdotal evidence supports the notion that many novice investors who attempt short-term speculation, or trading, lose a significant portion of their 'starting capital'.

Trading is not simply a matter of buying low and selling high. There is a great deal of work and research that needs to be conducted to develop the trading plan, select the trading tools, stick with the strategy, limit the losses on individual trades and manage your capital so that you are also maximising the potential returns.

Trading is also a risky business and should only be conducted with funds the investor is prepared to lose and that are not being relied upon for living requirements or debt repayment. For new investors it is generally not advisable to borrow money to trade — this is usually only considered by experienced investors. The reasons will be obvious as we progress through this chapter, particularly as we examine some of the common psychological hurdles that prevent many traders from reaching their goals.

Trading objectives and elements of success

Before you begin short-term speculation, or trading, you must be clear about why you want to trade. While trading to make a profit is the most valid reason, potential profits should be considered in light of the risk involved — in particular, volatility. This is because volatility can cause you to become an emotional trader rather than one who sticks to a system. As you will see, observing a few key principles of trading will help you resist giving into your emotions and increase your chances of success.

Why do you want to trade?

It is imperative that you define why it is you would like to trade. Ask yourself — what is the real reason you would like to trade? There are various reasons individuals are attracted to trading and some are outlined below.

Excitement

Many people who have seen the movies *Wall Street* and *Trading places* believe that trading is exciting and those who like to live close to the edge treat trading almost as a sport. The result is an attempt to 'beat the market'. This is the wrong reason to trade and indeed will probably lead to financial ruin. Successful trading is not very exciting. Successful trading requires a significant amount of time in the research and development phase, and relatively little time spent on executing orders. Once the strategy or methodology has been researched, tested and formalised, there is very little to get excited about. Orders are either written down or entered into a computer and faxed off to a broker or entered electronically. The trader then simply waits until his or her exit points are triggered and a new order is placed. To think of trading as exciting would suggest the approach is not correct.

Experience

Trading for the experience is acceptable provided the trader does not fall into the trap of needing to have a winning experience. Someone who is determining whether trading is truly suited to them should set out conservatively. For example, if you were to start with risk capital of $20,000, you may determine that if you lose 50 per cent through the experience, you will cease trading.

Trading for profit

This should be the main objective of trading. Attempting to trade for profit is a valid pursuit. Do not, however, expect to achieve a consistent profit immediately. There are hundreds of thousands of individuals who have traded for many years, have experienced the markets first-hand and are still trying to find the method that suits them best and is profitable. Very few people, if any, are profitable in trading immediately. Like any business, trading takes time to learn. Do not for one moment believe that trading will be a simple way for you to supplement your existing income. It won't be.

Maximising risk-adjusted returns

Traders should be aware that the goal is to make profits with relatively little risk. We are seeking to maximise our risk-adjusted returns. This goal suggests that we may ignore a trading method that has demonstrated a 2000 per cent return simply because the volatility of that return is too high. The following example will help illustrate the concept.

Suppose you are given the choice to pick one of two trading methods. One trading method provided a 140 per cent return, turning $10,000 into $24,000, while another trading method provided a 1900 per cent profit return on the initial investment. Which would you choose? The answer is self-evident. Of course you would go for the higher return.

Figure 12.1, below, shows the vastly different profits these rates of return would provide after one year.

Figure 12.1: Profit from two trading methods

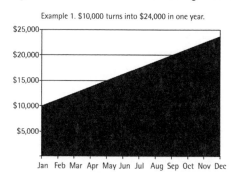

Example 1. $10,000 turns into $24,000 in one year.

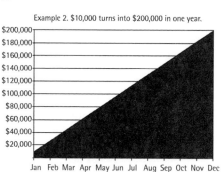

Example 2. $10,000 turns into $200,000 in one year.

What has not been illustrated in Figure 12.1 is the monthly variations in returns. While the graphs depict linear growth of the initial capital, this is not a true depiction of what went on during the year. Figure 12.2, overleaf, more realistically depicts the variations in the trader's equity during the year.

Figure 12.2: Monthly returns from two trading methods

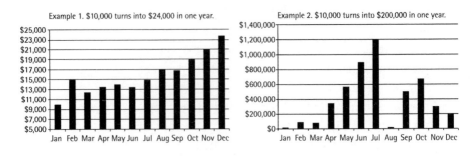

Example 1. $10,000 turns into $24,000 in one year.

Example 2. $10,000 turns into $200,000 in one year.

The two bar charts shown in Figure 12.2 are graphical representations of the same information as before. This time, however, the changes to the trader's equity throughout the year are shown. You can see that the equity using the second trading method did indeed rise from $10,000 to $200,000 by the end of the year. Notice that the original $10,000 at one point had grown to $1.2 million, but then was almost wiped out! The decline in equity was equivalent to a 98.3 per cent decline or loss. This would not be desirable.

Your initial reaction may be that you don't mind. Indeed some of you may be even more inclined to trade this method believing that if you start with $10,000 and it grows to $1.2 million, you will stop trading. Before getting too excited about this prospect, however, consider the possibility that you only started trading the system used in example 2 of Figure 12.2 in late July. Starting with $10,000, you have just wiped out 98 per cent. You now have just $170. You can forget what happened for the rest of the year, because with $170 you can no longer trade. You are out of the game.

Another reason we need to look at risk-adjusted returns is that lower volatility will result in closer adherence to the trading strategy. It is less likely that you will continue to trade a method after suffering a very big loss and so any positive returns after a substantial loss are less likely to be relevant because the trader is unlikely to be following the signals. The worst drawdown using the first trading method was comparatively low at just 16.6 per cent.

Remember — trading is complicated and difficult to achieve consistent success with. Perhaps that is why there are so few extremely profitable traders. Indeed, Warren Buffett once remarked, 'The stockmarket is just a big transfer mechanism; it transfers money from those who have no patience to those who do'.

Elements of success

If the activity of successful trading could be boiled down to its basic components, they would most likely include the following:

- have a plan and follow it
- let profits run
- cut losses short.

Have a plan and follow it

Like investing, no trading should be conducted unless it is part of a plan. Suppose your trading plan involves only trading stocks that meet certain fundamental criteria — such as you only trade stocks that are in the top 50 by market capitalisation. If you receive a call from a friend with a tip on a speculative stock opportunity where the stock is not part of the top 50, you have to ignore it. It is not part of your trading plan therefore it is not a trade you will be taking. If you have sufficient capital beyond that which is being dedicated to your trading methodology, you may take the tip; however, generally, you will not be entertaining outside influences of any description.

As mentioned in Chapter 1, by following a trading methodology, you will go through periods of poor performance, or drawdown. It is extremely difficult to continue trading a method that is not working well, particularly when someone you know is enjoying a solid period of growth at the same time you are suffering. The temptation will be to change your method or switch to a new method entirely. Don't. What you are experiencing now may simply be normal in terms of the trading system's behaviour.

There is no secret to trading success. A good plan, however, should include financial targets to tell you when to reduce your activity or reassess your plan.

Let profits run

Letting your profits run is also extremely difficult. While it should be part of your initial trading plan, it contains its own set of problems — mainly to do with emotions. Imagine you have been trading for some time and you have just had three losing trades in a row or perhaps more. The next trade, however, is working exceptionally well. The shares you bought are travelling higher and the news being released appears to be good. Without having experienced the losing trades, it may be difficult to imagine that you will now be very tempted to take some of the profits on this latest trade. The trader will justify the taking of profits because he or she does not want it to turn into another loss. The adage 'you can't go broke taking a profit' comes to mind.

Perhaps you have lost $3,000 on the last three trades and this trade is showing a $3,000 profit. Why not take the profit and completely offset those previous losses and 'start again' so to speak? Suppose you do sell and take the profit. You'll feel pretty smart for having done so, particularly if the next day the stock falls. Suppose, however, the next day the shares double in price and you could have earned $6,000 profit. Now you are well behind and if the next few trades are losing trades again, you can immediately see that you will be in a losing position instead of a winning position.

Cut losses short

Cutting losses short is perhaps even more important than letting your profits run. Clearly, while letting your profits run is desirable, they can only run so far. It is therefore important to keep the losses as small as possible to give the running profits a solid chance of increasing your equity beyond the losses incurred through the losing trades.

It may perhaps seem unusual to talk about losses. Isn't it true that if we are trading well, we won't have any losses?

Nothing could be further from the truth! Losing is part of the business of trading. Just as a business can have a poor trading week or month, the same will be true when trading markets and shares. You will have losing periods. Good trading is about recovering from the losses efficiently. It is easier to recover from losses if those losses are small.

Keeping losses small, however, is easier said than done. There are thousands of Australians holding onto losing stocks that they purchased months or even years ago. The only reason they are holding them is because they feel they have lost too much money now and are happy to hold on for as long as is needed for the share price to recover. Traders should never be in this situation. Before the loss gets to the point of no return, they should be exiting.

It is difficult to take losses. By taking a loss the trader is admitting he or she is wrong and most individuals find it difficult to admit a mistake. It is also difficult to take a loss if the trader has already taken a few and is being forced to take another. He or she may be forgiven for thinking the technique is not working. Remember — if the method has been researched thoroughly, the trader should not second-guess the system or method. If the trader is selecting which trades put up by the system will be taken and which will be ignored, the trader is not following the plan.

Perhaps the most important point is that if the trader does not take a small loss now he or she will be forced to take a larger loss later. It is important to be aware that taking losses is part of the business of trading. A good trader is not someone who never has a losing trade. A good trader is someone who, after taking a loss, has the fortitude to learn from the loss, continue trading and recover quickly.

You can have more losses than profits and still win

It is perhaps interesting to know that if the trader follows the rules regarding profits and losses, the number of winning trades can be less than the number of losing trades. Suppose the trader has developed a trading system that gets it right 30 per cent of the time. Notice that we are not even considering a success rate of above 50 per cent. The reality is that even excellent traders only get it right perhaps 40 per cent of the time. Trading systems that have a success rate of 80 per cent or 90 per cent are most likely unrealistic. Either the system doesn't get it right that often or, if it does, it takes so many trades that the trader could not possibly afford to take all the trades the system offers. Alternatively, the system has not been tested thoroughly enough.

A winning trader's profile

Figure 12.3, below, describes the last 10 trades of a trader who has a 30 per cent success rate. The three winning trades were each $100 while the seven losing trades were each just $10. You can see that with this kind of ratio between the size of the winning trades and the losing trades, the trader is well in front, despite only 'getting it right' less than one-third of the time.

Figure 12.3: Winning trader lets profits run and cuts losses

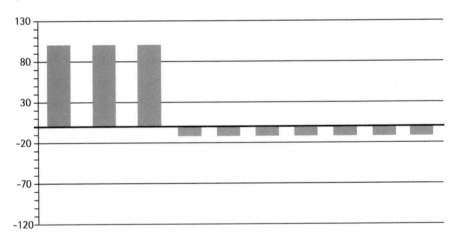

The emotional trader's profile

Now consider the emotional trader who lets his or her losing trades get bigger. Rather than sell shares that have fallen in price, he or she holds on, hoping that the price of the shares will recover. It keeps falling, however, and eventually the trader is forced to take a large loss. This doesn't just happen once, it occurs many times because as they say — hope springs eternal.

Conversely, the winning trades are kept small rather than let run, because the trader is afraid that the small wins will turn into large losses.

Figure 12.4: Emotional trader lets losses grow and takes profits early

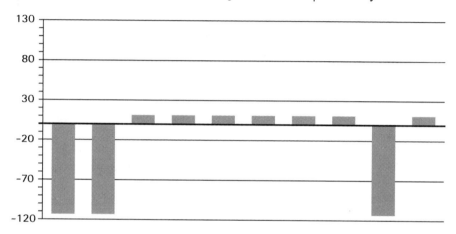

The emotional trader has ample opportunity to trade well. Indeed the system being used (but not followed properly) is showing a success rate of 70 per cent! There are 70 per cent winning trades and yet the emotional trader has lost money. By doing the opposite of what is required, he or she has let losses run and cut profits. The net result is a substantial loss. The trading method is important, but not nearly as important as the trader's ability to follow the trading method, keep losses small and let profits run.

Mechanical approaches to trading

A mechanical approach is an approach that can be quantified and its success measured. As you will see, some of the classic technical patterns are open to interpretation and so are more difficult, if not impossible, to measure the success (or otherwise) of. A mechanical approach is not subjective. That means that there is little or no interpretation of the rules that are used to enter or exit a trade. An example of a mechanical approach to trading may be:

- Entry rule: if the day is Monday buy 100 shares on open

- Exit rule: if an open position exists sell on close.

Notice that these rules are not subjective. There can be no personal interpretation that differs from anybody else's interpretation. If 100 people followed this method, they should also be placing the same orders at the same time. Compare these rules to the following.

- Entry rule: buy on a break of trendline resistance

- Exit rule: sell on a break of trendline support.

Support or resistance trendlines
Support trendlines are drawn at the price level at which falling share prices stop declining and move sideways or upwards because there is sufficient demand to stop the price from falling.

Resistance trendlines are drawn at the price level at which rising prices start moving sideways or down because there is an abbundance of supply.

What is the problem here? The obvious problem is that we don't know where the support or resistance trendline has been drawn. Different technical analysts may have different support and resistance levels and so the exact entry point is not clear. The exact exit point is also not clear. In the earlier example the entry was precise: if the day *is Monday*, you will *buy on open*. Simple.

Why take a mechanical approach?

There are several benefits to using a mechanical trading system or a mechanised approach. Indeed, traders should spend the majority of their time not trading, but building, assessing, testing and reassessing their mechanical approach. As mentioned, while this is not nearly as exciting as the images portrayed in movies such as *Wall Street* and *Trading places*, what the approach lacks in excitement it more than makes up for in the benefits outlined below.

A statistical edge

The main advantage of a mechanical approach to trading is what is referred to as a 'statistical edge' — indeed, this is the most important reason for using a trading system. A statistical edge means that after testing the system thoroughly, there exists a positive mathematical expectation from trading that system. Another method for calculating the statistical edge is to work out the average trade size. If it is large enough to cover all of the costs associated with trading and is still a positive number, it may make the system worth trading.

Objectivity

Trading is an extremely emotional activity. Unfortunately, no matter how often you are instructed to remove emotions from your trading decision, it is next to impossible for the beginning trader to achieve. A mechanical trading system, however, is a step in the right direction. A trading system allows you to combat subjective emotions with objectivity. The more objective you are the less likely you are to be influenced by news events, friends calling with 'hot tips' and fear and hope. All of these influences serve only one purpose, to stop you following your approach. A mechanical approach is clear, concise, and easy to follow. There is no interpretation, no subjectivity. The chances of you being unsure as to how to act are minimised. With a mechanised approach, when the signal arrives you will know exactly whether to buy or sell, the price at which to do so and what quantity to trade. With a mechanical approach, the fear about whether you should take the trade or not is taken away from you.

Consistency

Consistency in trading and investing is one of the hallmarks of the world's best. Warren Buffett consistently followed his strategy and did not suffer during the tech wreck of 2000. Peter Lynch, while running the Fidelity funds in the United States for 13 years from 1977, used a consistent method of evaluating companies to achieve an average annual return of 29 per cent and beat the S&P 500.

The markets will always rise and fall on rumours, speculation and irrational exuberance. A consistent approach cuts through the uncertainty and the illogical movements to locate the opportunities when they transpire.

Suppose you discovered that whenever the market closed higher than its open on Monday, the market rallied strongly on Tuesday — and that this happened 100 per cent of the time. In this case, it would be easy to apply a consistent approach — you would simply buy on or just before the close on Monday if it looked like the close would be higher. You could ignore all of the temptations of the day, such as the fears of the US Federal Reserve raising or lowering interest rates, speculation on BHP's or NAB's profit results, and simply buy on the close Monday.

Mechanical trading offers a rare consistency that can otherwise be difficult to achieve.

Diversification

The advantages of diversification remain as true for trading as they do for investing. Proper diversification provides for significantly lower volatility of price and lower risk. Returns may also be lower but what is lost in returns is more than made up for by the lower risk. If time and mental energy are spent constantly trying to decipher the markets, trading patterns and signals, economic events and news, there is little room to trade across different markets or different time frames. A mechanical approach allows the trader to easily diversify across markets, across time frames (short, medium or long term) and even across different trading systems. Perhaps the trader can run a trend following system and a non-trend or counter-trend system over the same market. Mechanising the trading approach provides a simple platform from which alternative strategies can be implemented.

Mechanical approach versus a random approach

Perhaps the easiest way of understanding the benefits of a mechanical trading system is to examine the alternative — a random approach. The random approach is often referred to as trading by the 'seat of the pants', or by 'gut feel' or 'intuitive' signs. While some traders use these methods with great success, it is often the case that they subconsciously have a more defined set of rules that must be met before they trade. These approaches, however, are not suitable for the aspiring trader.

Assume that a new trader has elected to follow a well thought out, well tested and thoroughly researched trading method. At the same time, another trader with equally little experience has begun to trade just using his intuition.

Both traders begin to risk real capital in the sharemarket and trade relatively frequently. The system trader is carefully following her system and does not deviate from the rules. The 'seat of the pants' trader, however, tries everything. He listens to his broker, follows the newspapers, reads magazines, subscribes to a newsletter. In the first six months, both traders have lost $10,000!

What happens next is very important. The random trader changes his broker, subscribes to a different newsletter and starts to chat online about trading and speculative stocks. The system trader, on the other hand, understands that a $10,000 loss is part of the landscape of her system and that historical testing revealed there was a good chance of such a drawdown. The system trader continues following the system.

Another six months pass and the system trader has recovered almost all of the drawdown. The random trader, however, continues to win a few and lose a few and stops trading altogether. The system trader keeps trading and is now in the black. She continues to win a few and lose a few but is following a carefully defined approach ensuring that her winning trades are larger than her losing trades.

Generally speaking, following a mechanical approach and learning that it does not work is preferable to following no approach at all. If you do not follow any approach at all and as a trader you do poorly, what have you learned? Nothing. Conversely, if you do well how can you have any confidence that you will be able to repeat your performance? You cannot. By not following a mechanical approach, you have learnt very little if anything from the experience. If, however, you follow a mechanical approach to trading and it works, you can have some confidence in the approach. If it doesn't work, you have at least learnt that you need to develop a new mechanical approach and that the current approach does not stand up to real-time trading.

Robust trading systems

Suppose you built a trading system and discovered that it made a million dollars on BHP but not a single cent on any other stock listed in Australia or in the United States. Would you trade that system just on BHP?

It is no use trading a mechanical system that worked on BHP shares over a particular historical three-year period. Even if that system made one million dollars during that period, if it has not worked in any other period or on any other shares, it probably won't work for you.

The system you use must be robust. A robust system should work on a variety of similar or different markets or shares and across different time frames.

Robust systems are not difficult to determine. Quite simply, robust systems, when systematically implemented over a long period of time and over many markets, tend to be profitable. They tend to enter in the direction of the trend, cut off losses quickly and let profits run. And these are elements of successful speculation.

Treat trading losses like errors

Speculation is a high-risk endeavour. As we noted earlier, some of the risks cannot be mitigated to any meaningful degree. Further, highly profitable trades are few and far between. When they do occur it is essential to let them progress to their fullest extent. Conversely, the frequency of losing trades can be high and, to avoid significant losses accruing, it is imperative that the trader prevents large losses transpiring by exiting as soon as practicable.

Perhaps an examination of the approach adopted by the institutions in the event of a 'mistake' can shed some light on how the private trader should approach losses — that is, consider all losing trades as errors. As mentioned, these errors are often best exited using a mechanical approach that exits the trade as soon as the error is discovered.

Having examined the benefits of a mechanical trading approach, as well as the approach to be adopted with individual losses, let's now look at an example of a mechanical trading system.

An example of a mechanical trading system

The mechanical trading system we are about to develop should only be seen as an example. Under no circumstances should this method be adopted without fully and correctly testing it. The process of testing a mechanical trading system is essential but convoluted, and it goes well beyond the scope of this book.

A mechanical trading system is simply a collection of rules that can be broadly classified as follows:

- entry signal rules, including:
    - entry trigger
    - entry filters
- exit signal rules, including:
    - exit trigger
    - exit filters
- rules for how much to risk in total
- rules for how much to risk per trade
- rules for how to change how much to risk
- rules for when to stop trading.

The examination of every section of the trading system development process extends beyond the boundaries of this book. Here we will examine an example of a mechanical entry and exit signal. The rest of the rules which are broadly described as money management rules are for further study.

In an attempt to avoid overwhelming you with reams of evidence and statistics to support various trading techniques and methods, we will simply look at one idea. This idea should serve to plant the seed of investigation and, for those interested, prompt a more avid examination of what is needed.

The entry signal

Every element of a trading technique must be based on logic. Simply buying because a red line crosses a blue line is not reason enough to risk real funds, even if those funds represent a small proportion of the overall funds invested.

Our example trading entry technique is based on price action. There is a technical filter and a price trigger. The job of the filter is not to generate more profitable trades, but to remove some of the losing trades. The removal of even one losing trade will improve the profitability of the trading technique overall.

Filter
A filter is a proviso built into a set of conditions that allows or stops certain actions being taken.

Simple moving average filter

The filter we will use is called a simple moving average. The simple moving average is quite easy to calculate. Add up the closing prices for the last 'n' days and then divide the total by 'n'.

For example, if n = 30, add together the closing prices for the last 30 days and divide the total by 30. The result will be the average price for the last 30 days.

The indicator, however, is called the moving average because the average moves forward a day at a time (or weekly or monthly, or even hourly). To move the average, simply include the latest closing price and drop off the oldest closing price which, continuing the above example, will now be 31 days old. You will be left with a new sample of 30 days that includes today's close.

One of the observations you will make is that the simple moving average 'follows' the price action. Figure 12.5, opposite, clearly illustrates this tendency.

You can clearly observe that as the price of the shares goes up, so does the moving average, and as the price of the shares falls, so does the moving average. By isolating the slope of the moving average, the trader is able to define a 'trend' for the underlying shares. That is, if the slope of the moving average is up, the shares are expected to be in an uptrend. If the slope of the moving average is negative, the shares are expected to be in a downtrend.

Figure 12.5: The simple moving average follows the share price

Defining the trend, however, is one part of the equation — the other is applying a filter. The moving average adequately helps to define a trend and provides a required filter. For this trading system, the filter works by only allowing trades when the trend is up. Any trades which are triggered when the moving average is in a downtrend will not be implemented.

The highest high trigger

The trading method also requires a trigger. The trigger will also be based on logic. The logic goes something like this: 'The shares cannot go up, without first going up.' Profound stuff, isn't it? Seriously though, the price of a share cannot rise from 10 cents up to $10 without first rising through 11 cents or 20 cents or $1. So the trigger used can be what's known as a highest high trigger. This shows the highest high over a set period of time.

Figure 12.6, overleaf, shows the highest highs looking back 20 days. The chart has a solid black line running above the prices. This line marks the level of the highest high looking back 20 days from the current day. This can be used to trigger a buy signal — that is, if the price of the share breaks and closes above the highest high, we will trigger an entry signal, but only when one other condition is also met. Remember — the moving average must also have an upward slope. If the moving average has a negative slope or is flat, no trade will be triggered even if prices break above the highest high.

Figure 12.6: Enter on breaks above the highest 20-day high

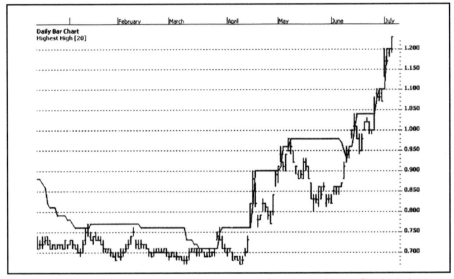

Source: Investors Advantage. Reproduced with permission.

The exit signals

The exit signal used can be the reverse of the entry signal. Alternatively, another technique or combination of indicators and price action can be used to trigger an exit trade. The exit signal may also be a particular price pattern such as a close in the lower quartile for the day's trading range. Finally, a profit and loss objective in actual dollar terms could be used (although we consider this method the least desirable for new traders). For our example, we will reverse our entry signals to produce our exit signals, meaning the moving average must be in a downtrend and we will use a lowest low indicator as our trigger.

In Figure 12.7, opposite, we have selected the lowest low indicator of the last 10 days. It shows where an exit may have occurred.

Figure 12.7: Exit on breaks below the lowest 10-day low

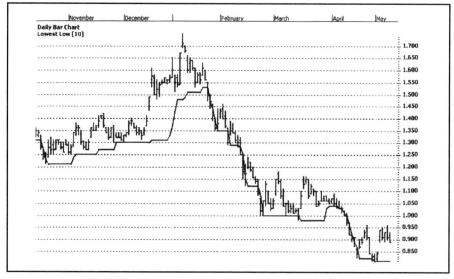

Source: Investors Advantage. Reproduced with permission.

The combination of the proposed entry technique which triggered an entry signal in January and exit rules which triggered an exit signal in October has produced a profitable trade. This, however, will not always be the case.

Remember — the goal is to allow the profitable trades to run for as long as possible and to reduce the adverse financial impact of a losing trade by exiting as soon as possible. The lowest low indicator is our signal that the previous uptrend may be ending.

As mentioned, this system would need to be rigorously checked to ensure it is robust before being used.

What to do with profits and losses

The speculating account was built to provide an avenue through which the speculative bug could be encouraged and given the best chance to prosper. The method we have outlined is by no means a certainty to make any profits at all.

If profits do accrue, however, we recommend for most traders that these are not ploughed back into the speculating account. Rather, every six or twelve months, a proportion of the profits generated in the speculating account should be fed back into the investing account. Profits are rare and in trading also often fleeting. Hold onto those profits by reallocating the funds to the investing account, which has been established to protect the long-term purchasing power of the investor.

And what about losses? A loss means reduced speculative activity until such time as the investing account provides excess returns again. It does not mean taking more funds out of the investing account. While this may result in a twelve-month wait, don't despair. Use the one-year hiatus to read and educate yourself — for example, by attending workshops on the subject and listening to guest speakers at the ASX investor events.

It is important to have a rule for when to cease speculating. A good rule of thumb is once a loss equates to 50 per cent of the funds being risked, trading should cease. Many of you at this point will realise that 50 per cent of the 25 per cent of any excess returns over a year will probably be a very small amount. Starting small, however, is the way to go and if it means you cannot afford to speculate, that is precisely the right choice to make — only when risk capital is significant, can small amounts of capital be risked.

Word of warning for traders

Trading is part science and a large part art. There are many dangers. The historical testing is based on previous data and probabilities based on this data are bound to change. There are costs in trading such as gaps and slippage that cannot be mitigated and there is the ever-present risk of loss. For these reasons trading is not for everyone and, as mentioned, investors should consider only risking money that they can afford to lose.

The purpose of classic technical analysis

As we have seen, a mechanical approach to trading, or 'quantitative technical analysis' as it is also called, can be measured and tested and so the results have a better chance of being reliable. Its counterpart — classic technical analysis — is more subjective.

Classic technical analysis is the study of charts and various patterns that are formed by those charts. The patterns have been given names such as head and shoulders tops, rounding bottoms, pennants, triangles, rising and falling wedges, Dojis, engulfing shadows and dark clouds. Some of these are useful in analysis when interpreted correctly but to the great majority of traders they provide little profitable benefit. Their subjectivity makes it difficult for the trader to consistently define, isolate and trade these patterns. To those with less experience in the 'art' of classic technical analysis, perhaps the more quantitative approach that we discussed above will prove more beneficial.

Limits to fundamental analysis for traders

Can fundamental analysis help with the problem highlighted in George Soros's model for reflexivity? You may recall the model we discussed in Chapter 5. We noted that as a company's earnings rose, so too did the share price. Unfortunately, it was also observed that, because the market looks ahead, the share price could fall even though earnings continued to rise if the market believes that 'future' earnings would be flat or lower.

To a certain extent fundamental analysis can help here. Perhaps a discussion with the board may reveal some concerns about the future growth in earnings. Perhaps the potential introduction of new technology by another company will add to competition and so slow growth or even result in a decline in earnings. Perhaps, however, there is no warning on the horizon. In this case, the stock simply begins to decline without apparent explanation. No doubt advisers and brokers in these circumstances would receive many phone calls from concerned investors wanting to know what was going on. Unfortunately, there may be nothing that the broker can see either. He or she looks at the current state of affairs, which reflect a rosy picture. Remember the Soros model — earnings have grown strongly in recent times and are continuing to grow. There appears to be no reason to be concerned and certainly nothing evident to justify selling the shareholding.

To the long-term investor, nothing appears to have changed. To the short-term trader, however, this company's shares are moving in the wrong direction! Something has definitely changed.

It is safe to say that there are limits to traditional approaches to fundamental analysis, even for the professional equity analyst. The fundamental analyst is looking at the past to determine the future. Unanticipated events occur frequently, even regularly. Fundamental analysis is as limited as anything else in attempting to predict the unpredictable. Accounting standards make certain measurements difficult to accurately obtain. As we highlighted earlier, the calculations used in fundamental analysis have limited abilities. For example, sales in current value dollars may be compared to assets that are valued on a historical basis. Apples are not being compared with apples and so assumptions are made. Many assumptions are incorrect or inappropriate and so the analysis becomes useless.

For traders, the limitations are even more obvious. While new data on a company may not be released for six months, the price of a company's shares changes every day. This raises the obvious question that something other than fundamentals are moving share prices in the shorter term.

Expectations

That 'something' moving share prices is expectations. Short-term expectations can move prices beyond reasonable levels — and indeed to ridiculous levels — both upwards and downwards. The share price will only remain at these extreme levels and will only continue in that direction if those short-term expectations are realised. The NetJ.com example used below may help explain.

Example: NetJ.Com — believe it or not

In late 1999 an internet staging company sought listing on the US OTCBB (Over The Counter Bulletin Board). In its Securities and Exchange Commission filing the company noted its business activities and its intentions:

> NetJ.Com conducts no business activity of any description. NetJ.Com also has no plans to conduct any business activity of any description.

The company has no business and no plans of having any business! The company sought 50 cents per share and listed on its first day at just under $2! That is nearly a 200 per cent gain. But if that is surprising, by March 2000 the stock was trading at $8!

How can fundamental analysis capture another almost 400 per cent rise in the share price? It can't. Now it may be reasonably argued that nobody in his or her right mind should invest in or trade the shares of this company. We have no argument there. The example, however, illustrates the limitation of fundamental analysis with regard to short-term price movements.

Advantages of fundamentals

There are over 1,600 companies listed on ASX. How are you going to follow them all? Alternatively, suppose you are given two buy signals according to your trading method. One of the companies is well supported by institutional research. This particular company has an excellent track record of growth, a history of paying higher dividends each year and solid profitability as measured by a number of different ratios. The other company you have been given a buy signal on has been trading at 3 cents for years. There is no formal research on this company and all you have found out is that there is a rumour floating around suggesting the company may be making an investment in a new and exciting venture. Which buy signal would you take? Both stocks could do well for the trader.

Fundamental analysis can highlight companies with quality businesses, quality management, a strong growth history and strong profitability. Perhaps you have decided that it is simply too difficult to watch all of the companies listed on the ASX. Fundamental analysis can then be used to reduce the universe of stocks you are going to watch and focus your attention on those companies with strong fundamental merits.

So fundamental analysis has a significant use in selecting which shares to trade. Fundamental analysis, however, cannot usually help us with short-term direction. Technical analysis (or a mechanical approach) therefore can be used in the speculating account to help us answer the question of when to trade.

Economic fundamentals

Understanding economic factors and how they relate to the markets is vital. While this course advocates the use of a more mechanical approach to trading, an understanding of the influences on the market and on individual share prices is extremely important.

Interest rates

If all roads lead to Rome, in the world of finance and economics, Rome is interest rates. Interest rates have a threefold impact on the stock market. This is because interest rates affect:

- profits and profitability of a corporation
- relative returns of different investments
- borrowing costs associated with making a sharemarket investment.

Interest rates and profits

A corporation incurs many expenses as part of its ongoing business activity. For example, if it has borrowed any money to purchase inventory or fund expansion through organic growth or acquisition, that company will have an interest expense. The interest expense will reduce profits of the company, which in itself is not a bad thing. Indeed, lower profits may be desirable because lower taxes will be paid. A simplified profit and loss statement, shown in Table 12.1, below, will illustrate the advantage of lowering taxes through the use of borrowings to fund a company's plans.

Table 12.1: Statement of financial performance for ACME Asset Management Ltd

Sales Revenue	10,000,000
Cost of Goods Sold	6,100,000
Gross Profit	3,900,000
Other Expenses	
Depreciation	200,000
Amortisation	300,000
Interest	400,000
Net Profit Before Tax	3,000,000
Taxation Expense	900,000
Net Profit After Tax	2,100,000

After the taxes are paid, part of the net profits may be distributed among the shareholders by way of a dividend. For many investors these dividends are an essential component of their returns. Indeed, investors should remember that when a share is purchased, what is really being bought is a 'right' to share in the income generated from the ownership of that share.

If the income is expected to rise, purchasers of that right are more willing to pay a higher price, meaning the value of each share or right rises. If, on the other hand, the future income is expected to decline, the price of that share would fall, as investors would be less willing to purchase the shares.

Therefore, if interest rates rise and the profits of a company fall (all things being equal), we would expect the price of shares to fall. So it is that rising interest rates are viewed as negative for the market.

Investment relatives

Suppose an investor has his funds tied up in bank bills or a term deposit. When that investment matures, if interest rates in the marketplace have fallen, the interest rate he receives should he 'roll' his investment for another period will be lower. In this situation, because the return on interest-bearing investments has declined, investors may be more inclined to switch out of 'cash' investments into the stock market. Conversely, if interest rates are rising, investors may be more inclined to move their funds out of the stock market and into cash-style investments as the returns are improving and there is lower volatility and risk associated with such investments. Under this scenario, the stock market may fall as a result of rising interest rates.

As they search for the best risk-adjusted return, investors may sell stocks and buy cash investments if interest rates rise. This flow of funds between investment classes occurs constantly among institutional investors as they re-weight their portfolios in an attempt to achieve high risk-adjusted returns. As a result of their activities, the relative valuations of the market change and so too the level of the market.

Cost of investment loans

A relative newcomer to the list of ways in which interest rates can affect the stockmarket is margin lending, or the act of borrowing money to finance a purchase of shares.

Margin lending became popular and more widespread in the 1990s as investors began to understand the advantages of leverage. Indeed, as investors searched for techniques to improve returns, many turned a blind eye to the added risks that were being assumed. Regardless, the offer of funds to purchase more shares than what could otherwise be bought raises the level of prices in the market, as there is simply more money being funnelled into it. If interest rates rise, however, investors become less inclined to borrow money to buy shares and so the support that existed previously is removed. Less demand for a given level of supply is negative and so higher interest rates may result in the market falling.

In summary, higher interest rates are generally a negative influence on the market for three major reasons. Higher interest rates reduce profits of corporations, making their shares a less desirable investment at the current price. Higher interest rates make cash investments a more attractive alternative and so funds switch from the stock market into cash or similar investments. This action of selling out of the stock market can push the market lower. Finally, higher interest rates reduce the demand for margin lending products and so this area of support for the market is removed, again possibly pushing the market lower.

What causes interest rates to change?

Interest rate management is called monetary policy. One of the purposes of monetary policy as used by the Reserve Bank of Australia (RBA) is to control inflation. While the government sets the objectives of monetary policy, it is the RBA that enacts the mechanical aspects of the policy to change interest rates.

Monetary policy
Monetary policy is government policy regarding the supply of money and interest rates. It is now usually conducted at 'arm's length' by a central bank.

The RBA does this through changes to the supply of cash in the market, using its open market operations (OMO). OMO is the activity of buying and selling government securities and repurchase agreements to change the level of cash in the market. A lower amount of cash in the market would raise the price of that cash. The price of money is the interest rate and so if the price of cash rises because the government is less willing to buy securities and inject cash into the market, the interest rate will rise.

The basic objective of the RBA is contained in the *Reserve Bank Act 1959 (Cth)*. The act gives the RBA the responsibility of achieving price stability and promoting the economic prosperity and welfare of Australians.

We can assume that this means low inflation and a sustainable and desirable rate of economic growth. It is important to keep inflation down and understanding the link between inflation and interest rates can help traders understand the markets.

Inflation

Inflation measures the extent to which the prices of a basket of consumer goods and services are rising. Some inflation is desirable as rising prices provide the opportunity for company profits to grow. In turn, increased profits mean the company may employ more people, which adds to economic prosperity. High inflation, however, is undesirable as it reduces the purchasing power of everyone, particularly those on fixed incomes such as those on the various forms of social security. Declining purchasing power is tantamount to a decline in the quality of living. It is in the governments' best interests to maintain or raise the standard of living of its constituents.

One way to combat high inflation is to raise interest rates. Raising interest rates, through increasing the cost of borrowing funds needed to invest, slows investment spending. This leads to lower levels of employment growth and wage rises and, in turn, lower levels of consumer spending and general economic expansion. This reduces the demand for goods and services and so reduces pressure on prices.

From the trader's perspective, if economic indicators suggest an economic acceleration that may lead to higher prices, there could be talk of a potential interest rate rise. While different sectors of the market will react at different times to the prospect of higher interest rates, as shown above, the generally accepted view is that higher rates are not positive for the market.

All economic statistics are taken into consideration by the RBA when formulating its policy stance. These may include:

- inflation
- gross domestic product — a measure of economic growth
- the level of the Australian dollar
- international interest rate levels — particularly those in the United States

- unemployment
- housing starts
- car registrations
- retail sales
- wages
- fiscal policy and taxes
- competition policy.

Beyond a simplistic analysis of the various ways interest rates impact on the stockmarket, there are the various combinations between interest rates rising or falling, economic growth rising or declining, and inflation stable, rising or falling that all create different outcomes. The study of these combinations takes us well beyond the scope of this book. Suffice to say, however, that the stock market is always looking ahead at least six months.

People interested in studying longer term investment strategies that employ fundamental analysis and the study of the economy should attend ASX's Easy Steps to Share Investment course and, in particular, should attend module three 'Analysing and selecting shares'.

Your own strategy is most critical

Based on errors made in the past, it would appear that economists, market strategists and journalists can only be about as broadly correct as we ourselves can be. So if we can't rely on the experts for consistently accurate forecasts, why do we spend so much money on magazines, newspapers and newsletters? Who can we turn to for reliable information about investing and the markets?

Many investors heavily rely on the efforts of self-professed experts. They buy the magazines and read them from cover to cover. They believe the selective claims made about the stock picking ability of various newsletter authors and subscribe for a year, believing they will help them become millionaires just like the authors. Interestingly, the ratio of successful traders and investors to unsuccessful ones is identical among those who read these publications and those who do not. Clearly the publications are doing very little to increase the chances of success. So why subscribe?

The need for information appears to be the driving force. This justification is rational and logical. Traders believe that they do not know enough and that the more well informed they can make themselves about current market circumstances and 'hot stocks to watch', the better their chances of hitting the home run will be. However, the subscriptions are being used merely as a crutch and are not likely to increase the chances of success.

It is correct to seek knowledge, but the knowledge that is needed is how to develop your own strategy. Once the strategy has been developed, tested, formalised and implemented, the trader is free to read the magazines and newsletters objectively and may indeed use the information they contain to reinforce decisions that have already been made.

Pulling it all together

This chapter gives an overview of Part I to help you on your way to successful investing and trading. To become a successful investor and trader, there are 10 pillars that need to be remembered and followed. They are:

- determine what type of investor you are
- think long term
- be disciplined
- diversify with a purpose
- be objective
- organise your goals
- build separate investing and speculating accounts
- develop a long-term stock selection strategy
- develop a mechanical approach to short-term trading
- begin.

We will review these in more detail below.

Determine what type of investor you are

The type of investor you are will determine the approach that suits you. Your attitude to risk in particular will determine the proportion of growth assets you can handle in your portfolio. The higher the proportion of growth assets (such as shares), the greater the relative volatility of returns you will experience will be. Also remember our thoughts on short-term volatility — that is, the longer you invest, the lower the volatility.

Think long term

It is true that over the long term, the sharemarket has outperformed most other asset classes. However, as most investors like to select their own shares, there is a strong chance that returns will not be the same as that of the overall index. Therefore, when convincing yourself of the benefits of investing long term, it pays to remember the fact that volatility takes care of itself as the years pass. What seem like huge movements today may appear to be minor hiccups when viewed through the looking glass of a long-term time frame. Further, over long periods of time, the market is remarkably stable when viewed from the perspective of the returns from a solid business. A solid business tends to have reliable earnings and distributions over time in contrast to the short-term fluctuations in the price of the company's shares, which are driven by emotion, impatience and greed.

The benefits of compounding also accrue for the long-term investor. As time passes, earnings generate more earnings and the result is an exponential rise in the value of the investment and the income that is generated from it.

Be disciplined

Effective investing is almost impossible without a consistent and methodical approach. Greed, fear and hope all conspire to thwart any attempt at rational decision making. For this reason, an approach founded on rigorous consistency — a disciplined approach — will ensure you don't stray from the plan you have set for yourself. Even though the plan or strategy may go through periods of underperformance or it may seem to be taking an eternity to build profits, it is essential you stick with it. Failure to follow the strategy through to its conclusion means that, for most investors, there is virtually no chance of reaching true financial independence — tax and inflation will see to that.

Diversify with a purpose

Diversification serves primarily to protect the overall investment return. That is, while one element of the investment is doing poorly, some other investment may be doing well and therefore offset the adverse impact of the poorly performing investment. Importantly, proper diversification doesn't simply serve to have the gain on one investment compensate for the loss on the other. Effective diversification should also see the total investment advance in value. Being aware that no investment will necessarily do well at all times can help force the investor to adopt a diversified approach.

Diversification has become almost a cliché, but proper diversification provides an opportunity for lower volatility without a significant negative effect on returns. The net result is higher risk-adjusted returns. There are, however, risks in diversifying too broadly. Diversification that is too wide can unnecessarily increase transaction costs and produce mediocre returns over the long term.

Be objective

Objectivity is the hallmark of all of the world's best investors. Emotions have little or no place in the investing process. It is emotions that see the stockmarket reach euphoric highs and then fall to depressing lows. A dispassionate approach to investing and assessing investment options is the only way to remain objective and assess options on their merits.

Organise your goals

Not everyone should trade or speculate. Those with only small amounts of capital and those who would regard themselves as risk averse should not speculate. If you do wish to speculate, approach the investment as you would any business in which your entire capital was at risk, rather than just a small part of it.

Know what stage of life you are in and ensure your investment goals and priorities are part of your investment strategy.

Build separate investing and speculating accounts

Creating separate investing and speculating accounts means having separate funds for each. Funds used in speculative trading should only be funds that you are prepared to lose. Only move returns over from your investing account into your speculating account that are in excess of the return benchmark you have set for your investing account — for example, a return benchmark of 15 per cent. Only use a quarter of excess returns for speculating and move profits from your speculating account back to your investing account to lock in profits and take advantage of the benefits of compounding returns.

Make regular contributions to your speculating account as you can and use dollar cost averaging to add to the portfolio over time. Cut your losses short and let your profits run.

Develop a stock selection strategy

Choose several models that work best for you and provide diversification by exposing the portfolio to growth potential regardless of whether the market is rewarding value or growth shares.

Develop a mechanical approach to trading

A mechanical approach has many advantages, including increasing the ability to have the results quantified on a continuous basis, removing subjectivity and, importantly, providing consistency.

Begin

Now you are ready to begin — good luck! Begin the process today. The longer you wait, the longer it will take for the benefits of compounding to provide their beneficial effect. We hope that this book has provided a more concrete approach to investing for the longer term. Your success, however, will very much depend on the quality of the shares you select for your portfolio. For this reason it is important that you learn as much about developing strategies and analysing businesses as possible. If you wish to read further, there are many books available. If you are the sort of person who prefers to listen rather than read, there are a number of advanced courses available through ASX or various reputable organisations.

Speak to the ASX education department for more information on ASX courses or go to the ASX wesite (www.asx.com.au).

Part II
Trading as part of the bigger picture

It is important to remember that trading shares on the Australian sharemarket should be one component of a focused wealth creation strategy, which takes into account your individual circumstances and goals. In this second part of the book we see how share trading fits into your overall financial plan.

Share trading decisions should be made in the context of your overall wealth creation strategy, and taxation and other compliance issues cannot be ignored. As more and more investors are managing their own superannuation funds, we also consider how to set up a self-managed superannuation fund and how share trading can play a part in building your retirement savings.

14

Understanding investment alternatives

Although most readers will have a particular interest in the sharemarket, it is important to understand investment alternatives — most of which will find a place in your investment portfolio at some time or another. This chapter will provide a brief overview of the investment alternatives to shares available.

When building the framework of your portfolio, within your share strategy, consideration should also be given to investing in some or all of the following main asset classes:

- cash
- interest-bearing investments
- property.

Cash and interest-bearing investments

Cash

The features of cash include:

- it usually provides the highest liquidity with the lowest risk
- it has zero growth
- it generally has no tax efficiency.

Cash management trusts have the potential to provide a higher return than a traditional bank account, and they are useful for 'parking' your money between investments.

Fixed and floating rate investments include:

- fixed and floating rate cash deposit accounts, such as:
    - bank deposits
    - building society accounts
    - credit union accounts
    - merchant bank accounts
- cash management trusts/accounts
- mortgages.

Investment considerations

Factors to take into account when considering how much of your portfolio to allocate to cash include:

- cash and interest-bearing investments provide security for your investment capital and easy access to your cash reserves
- staggered maturity dates allow flexibility for future investment
- regular interest payments aid cash flow planning
- as most offer no or little capital growth, they do not protect against inflation
- interest income is subject to income tax at your marginal tax rate.

Interest-bearing investments

The features of interest-bearing investments include:

- they provide a steady income stream
- they usually give a greater yield/interest than cash
- they offer either fixed or floating rates of interest

- they allow you to diversify your portfolio and reduce your risk

- the liquidity provided varies depending on the type of security and the market it is in

- both the payment stream and any capital gain is likely to be treated as income

- changing interest rates and company status can change the value of the security.

You can access interest-bearing securities through ASX. Some examples of interest-bearing investments are:

- Government bonds.

- Bank bills — which usually have a three- to six-month term with interest paid at maturity.

- Debentures — which are loans to companies at a fixed rate of interest and for a fixed term (usually one to five years), which are secured by a trust deed over an asset, or assets, of a company.

- Corporate bonds or unsecured notes — which are issued by financial institutions and companies for periods between three months and five years, and offer a higher rate of interest than other interest rate products of the same maturity as they are unsecured.

- Floating rate notes — which are issued by similar entities as unsecured notes and return an interest amount that is determined by market interest rates (usually the bank bill rate). These securities may be perpetual, meaning they do not have a specific maturity date and investors enter or exit the market by buying and selling on the ASX.

- Convertible notes — which are securities that pay you interest like a bond but are convertible into ordinary shares of a company at a prescribed price or ratio at specified times and/or at maturity.

- Hybrid securities — which are securities that are very similar to convertible notes, but which pay a franked or unfranked dividend instead of interest at a fixed or resettable rate. They are convertible into ordinary shares of a company at a prescribed price or ratio at a specified times and/or at maturity.
- Bond trusts.
- Fixed-term deposits.

The role of interest-bearing investments

Interest-bearing investments entitle the investor to a predetermined fixed or floating rate of return and repayment of a capital sum on a fixed date. These securities are sometimes described as income investments because generally they provide a steady and relatively high income return.

Interest-bearing investments can be useful as a stabilising influence on an investment portfolio and can reduce overall risk. These products can also be used as temporary havens in which excess cash or new funds may be placed to earn interest while you wait for other investment opportunities to arise.

When investing in unsecured notes, debentures or mortgages, it is important to spread your investments (and therefore your risk) across a number of companies and different industries. There should also be a spread of maturities so that any changes in the interest rates do not impact too heavily on your overall return.

Government bonds

Market interest rates and credit worthiness are the primary influence on the value of a bond (due to the inverse relationship between yield and price). When investors purchase a bond and interest rates fall, the capital value of that bond will increase. Conversely, if rates rise, existing bond prices will fall.

Most bonds carry a set interest rate (the coupon rate) which is paid at regular intervals, usually every six months, until the bond reaches maturity (the date the face value of the bond is repaid). It is important to understand that coupon rates (interest rates) for fixed rate bonds do not change after they are issued. Although the real value of money may change over time due to market interest rates and inflation, the actual income flow will not.

The amount originally invested in a bond (usually in multiples of $100) is called the face value. However, you may purchase a bond for more or less than its face value. The price depends on how much investors are willing to pay to earn the interest income provided by the bond. In other words, the coupon rate (or interest rate) is usually fixed, but the market price of the bond can move up and down.

For example, say you purchase a $100 bond that pays 8 per cent interest semiannually and is scheduled to mature in 10 years. Two years later, you decide to sell your bond. If by then interest rates on new bonds have fallen to 7 per cent, you will receive more than $100 when you sell your bond. Because an investor could now receive only 7 per cent from a new bond but your old bond still pays 8 per cent interest, your bond is now worth about $106. The gain in price of the bond has nothing to do with the quality of the bond — it is solely due to falling interest rates.

If, however, you decide to hold the bond for 10 years until maturity, you will receive your full $100 back and the interest that would be paid during the life of the bond.

The rule to remember is that bond prices move in an inverse manner to interest rates. If you bought a $10,000 face value bond with an 8 per cent coupon for less than $10,000 (for example, $9,000), your investment yield is higher than 8 per cent. If interest rates subsequently fall to 7 per cent, you could sell the bond for more than you paid for it.

A credit rating is given to most issued securities and also to the issuers of those securities. A downgrade or upgrade of these ratings will also either adversely or positively affect the capital value of these bonds.

Property

The features of property as an asset class include:

- it is a tangible asset
- it usually has low liquidity and is a variable risk
- it provides variable growth (and so has potential for loss or gain)
- over the long term, it can provide moderate to high income returns
- there are several classifications to choose from, including residential, commercial, industrial and retail
- it is usually a tax-effective investment.

People can lose money in real estate for the following reasons:

- They buy in an area which is not growing in value. This may be due to a number of factors such as slow employment growth, which reduces the demand for real estate from both tenants and buyers.
- They buy at inflated prices after a boom cycle.
- They overextend themselves by committing to loan payments that are too high for their circumstances.
- Their initial selection is poor. Remember the three golden rules when buying real estate — location, location and location.

Property can be held in a portfolio in several forms:

- home ownership for security
- direct property investment bought for capital gains and income
- indirect property investment through a listed or unlisted property trust.

Generally, direct investment involves the commitment of substantial amounts of capital, and is an illiquid investment.

Also, a property cannot be sold in parts — that is, you can't just sell the kitchen.

Unlisted property trusts

The features of unlisted property trusts include:

- the fund manager determines the portfolio
- there is usually a high cash component retained in case of redemptions — that is, the fund is not fully invested
- liquidity — that is, the manager's ability to repurchase — can vary depending on market conditions
- they have the ability to be a fund of funds — for example, a fund that invests in listed property trusts, which can be useful for smaller investors seeking greater diversification
- they will usually provide a relatively high yield with moderate growth.

Listed property trusts

The features of listed property trusts include:

- there are specific classes available, including retail, commercial, industrial and CBD
- they usually have high liquidity as they are traded on the ASX
- they generally provide high yield with good tax efficiency and moderate growth
- they can represent good value when trading at a discount to net tangible assets
- they are usually less volatile than other types of shares as they are held by investors mainly for income purposes.

Investment considerations

Things to consider when looking at property as an investment include:

■ it is a tangible asset that you can use yourself or improve to enhance returns

■ location is important

■ capital gains from property investments (other than your family home) are subject to capital gains tax after indexation for inflation

■ rent and other income is subject to income tax at your marginal tax rate

■ there is an opportunity for negative gearing

■ it is an illiquid asset — that is, it may take some time to sell your investment

■ a portion of the property cannot usually be sold in isolation.

Managed versus direct investments

There are a number of ways you can invest in each asset class. A working understanding of the alternatives available to you will simplify the process.

For example, let's consider the choices available with share investment. You can invest in one or more of the companies listed on the stock exchange. Or you can invest in any of the various products offered by the managed funds industry. The managed funds industry is a general name for that part of the financial sector which deals with the common ownership (and trading) of assets and securities through specially established funds. When investing in managed funds, the investor delegates the investment decisions and management to a third party — the fund manager. These funds pool investors' money to enable them to collectively purchase assets that individual investors may have difficulty acquiring for themselves.

Direct versus indirect investment

Investments in individual asset classes can be made either directly through the purchase of assets by the individual, or indirectly through investments in managed funds. The managers of these funds invest your capital in one or a combination of the major asset classes. In the following paragraphs, the pros and cons of direct and indirect investment have been summarised to help you to decide which ones suit you best. Your investment goals, risk profile, experience and the amount you have to invest will influence whether it is better to invest directly or indirectly in fixed interest, property or shares. For example, you may choose to invest directly in Australian shares, while investing indirectly in international shares to achieve greater diversity. A balanced portfolio will often have a blend of direct and indirect investments.

Direct investments

When an investor makes a direct investment, he or she purchases a specific share, property or fixed-interest product. For example, a direct investment in shares may involve the investor purchasing shares in BHP-Billiton or Coca-Cola Amatil Ltd.

Why invest directly?

Direct investment gives the investor control over those assets and investments, including the making of decisions relating to their day-to-day management and administration. Accordingly, direct investment will suit those investors with the time and expertise required to manage their own affairs, either by themselves, or in conjunction with an adviser.

Indirect (managed) investments

Investments can also be made indirectly by buying units in a managed fund. Typically, managed funds have five main features:

- investors pool their money to purchase assets collectively
- funds are invested, managed and administered by a promoter or manager

- investors delegate the investment decisions and day-to-day management of their funds to the manager
- investors collectively share in the risks associated with the investments of those funds
- managed investments are strictly governed by various acts and bodies.

Non-superannuation managed funds are governed by the *Managed Investments Act 1998*, which stipulates rigorous disclosure and compliance procedures. The legislation is administered by ASIC. Life products or superannuation products are regulated under the *Superannuation Industry (Supervision) Act 1993*. This legislation is jointly administered by ASIC, Australian Prudential Regulation Authority (APRA) and the Australian Taxation Office (ATO).

Most Australians are already indirect investors in the sharemarket thanks to the near universal membership of occupational superannuation and retirement funds, most of which invest a substantial proportion of their funds in shares.

Also, changes to the way people can prepare for their financial future have resulted in a dramatic increase in the number of self-managed superannuation funds. This fund structure allows investors to take direct control of their investment decisions and to invest more directly in the sharemarket.

More information about superannuation is included in Chapter 16.

Managed investments include unit trusts, insurance bonds, superannuation bonds, annuities and allocated pensions. Investors are able to purchase units in the fund and then rely on the manager's expertise to fulfil their needs, along with the needs of all the other investors in the fund.

Annuities and allocated pensions are discussed in greater detail in Chapter 18.

Typically, the cost of a managed investment includes one or more of the following:

- entry costs of 1 to 4 per cent of the investment amount
- nil entry with withdrawal penalties
- ongoing costs of 1.0 per cent to 2.5 per cent per annum.

Other common characteristics of managed investments include:

- the fund may be broad based or sector specific, local or international

- the fund may be diversified across asset classes and within an asset class

- the individuals within the management company may vary over time

- the fund size can range from one or two million dollars under management to several hundreds of millions of dollars

- the fund may aim to provide income or growth, or a combination of both, with a moderate degree of volatility relative to the market concerned.

Types of managed investments

There are many forms of managed investments, but they can be loosely categorised as follows:

- rollover funds — such as approved deposit funds (ADFs), deferred annuities (DAs), annuities, allocated pensions and superannuation bonds

- regular premium insurance and superannuation funds

- trusts, which can include:

  - equity (industrial and resources shares, overseas)

  - mortgage or property

  - bonds (both domestic and international)

  - currency (including options and futures)

  - insurance bonds

  - friendly society bonds.

Trusts are discussed in greater detail below.

Listed versus unlisted equity investments

Trusts offer a range of investments to the public. Their function is to attract and pool the funds of small, medium and large investors who wish to leave the decision making to investment professionals employed by recognised financial institutions. Generally, trusts are either listed or unlisted.

As the name implies, listed equity investments are managed equity trusts or companies quoted on the stock exchange. A number of features distinguish listed equity investments from their unlisted counterparts:

- Listed equity investments are typically company structures, meaning they have the ability to retain earnings and grow shareholders' wealth over time. Listed equity trusts have been allowed to also take advantage of the 12 months capital gains concession available to individuals. Unlisted equity investments are usually unit trusts and are therefore generally required by their governing documents to distribute nearly all of their earnings to unit holders. However, unlisted trusts have had a history of much greater volatility in terms of their distributions when compared to listed trusts.

- Listed equity investments have the advantage of a continuous trading market while unlisted alternatives require you to make a redemption request through the manager. The manager must therefore ensure that adequate cash reserves are available to redeem units when people decide to sell all or part of their holding in the trust.

- Listed equity investments are subject to market forces and can trade above or below their asset backing, whereas unlisted funds are usually purchased and redeemed at their net tangible asset backing.

Examples of listed managed equity investment companies and their ASX codes include Argo Investments Ltd (ARG), Australian Foundation Investment Company Ltd (AFI),

Whitefield Investments (WHF), Templeton Growth (TGG) and Choiseul Ltd (CHO).

Unlisted trusts are not listed on ASX but their values are generally quoted weekly in the financial press. They are offered to investors via a prospectus issued by the fund manager that outlines the investment criteria of the trust.

Returns for most types of trusts or funds are usually not guaranteed, but investments in trusts are expected to offer income and capital growth. Investors have the advantage of investing across a range of securities and management styles.

Currency, options and futures funds are sometimes capital guaranteed at maturity and are normally income-generating investments. They also provide the opportunity to invest in the more speculative areas of the market with limited risk.

Unlisted trusts traditionally have a higher cost structure than their listed alternatives. The annual management fee charged by the fund manager is usually more than that for listed trusts and represents a percentage of funds under management. The longer established listed investment companies such as AFI and ARG generally treat management costs as a company expense.

Investments in unlisted trusts can only be traded (bought and sold) through the fund manager, while listed trusts are easily bought and sold through a stockbroker. The tax and other benefits of listed and unlisted trusts depend on your individual circumstances, so it would be wise to seek advice before investing.

16 Superannuation funds

Superannuation funds can provide an attractive avenue for saving for retirement, particularly as these types of funds only pay 15 per cent tax on their net investment earnings. A superannuation fund can take the form of a trust or life office policy, and you can contribute to your retirement in a variety of ways.

Managed superannuation funds

In managed superannuation funds — which include retail and company/employer-sponsored funds — whether you or your employer contribute, the funds are pooled with other investors and invested by a fund manager in the various investment sectors. You can make regular contributions or a single lump sum payment. Flexibility in how you contribute and how your funds are allocated is often a key feature.

Advantages of managed superannuation funds

The most obvious advantage of employer-sponsored funds is their ease of use. Since the 1992 *Superannuation Guarantee (Administration) Act*, superannuation contributions made by employers on behalf of employees have been compulsory, and most employers will already have an arrangement set up for new employees.

Other advantages of managed superannuation funds include:

- At the time of writing, employers must contribute 9 per cent of the earnings of all employees receiving more than $450 per calendar month to their superannuation account. Most funds allow the employee to make additional contributions.

- Death and disability cover is often provided as part of the fund.

- The trustee of the fund is responsible for the efficient completion of all the administrative and compliance tasks associated with the fund's management.

- The large size of company funds facilitates the creation of more diverse investment portfolios.

- Many funds provide you with a number of options when it comes to distributing your investment capital across the various asset classes.

Disadvantages of managed superannuation funds

Disadvantages of managed funds include:

- You may be charged a management fee based on the amount of funds under management (for example, for retail funds you may be charged between 0.5 and 2 per cent).

- They have limited portability. This means it is possible to end up with small amounts of contributions in numerous funds as you move from job to job. A fee is then charged to consolidate these amounts into one fund.

- You have little control over exactly how and when your funds will be invested.

Self-managed superannuation funds

Self-managed superannuation funds are privately run funds established via a trust instrument that sets out how each fund is to operate and who the members and trustees are.

Advantages of self-managed superannuation funds

The advantages of self-managed superannuation funds include:

- Control — that is, you choose how your assets are invested, you monitor how those investments perform and you make further investment decisions based on that information.

- Flexibility — you can consider a range of investments that suits you and you can make corrections very quickly. You can also link your fund to your overall financial plan. Finally, when you reach retirement age, there is no need to close the fund, as you may choose to create a tax-effective income stream from your own fund by receiving that income as an allocated pension.

- Tax savings — the tax rate for income for superannuation funds is 15 per cent at the time of writing. Captal gains tax is levied at 15 per cent for assets held for less than 12 months and at 10 per cent for assets held for longer than 12 months. With a self-managed fund, you are in a better position to plan your investments in order to reduce the fund's overall tax rate. You may even be able to reduce the total tax payable by your fund to an effective rate of zero through the use of franking credits attached to dividends from shares held by the fund.

- Portability — self-managed funds follow you from job to job or contract to contract (if each new employer lets you choose the fund your contributions will be made into).

- Extended life — properly set up funds can provide ongoing benefits to your spouse and children for the same initial establishment costs.

Disadvantages of self-managed superannuation funds

As with most things, there are also disadvantages associated with self-managed superannuation funds, including:

- Responsibility for all decision making — decisions regarding asset allocation and stock selection rests with the fund trustees (within the outlines of the trust instrument), who must be members of the fund. (There is a type of DIY fund, known as an APRA fund, that allows you to appoint a professional trustee to run the fund on your behalf.)

- Responsibility for all administrative and compliance tasks — each self-managed fund must complete all the relevant administrative and compliance tasks. For this, the use of a professional adviser is recommended.

- Limited ability to diversify investments — due to their smaller size, self-managed superannuation funds are often limited in the number of investments they can hold compared to public funds.

- Trustees must keep up to date — the onus is on trustees to keep up to date with the rules and regulations affecting superannuation investments. Even if an adviser in this area is used, the ultimate responsibility remains with the trustees.

- Expense — depending on the types of investments held, or even the type of administration or trustee services used, managing and investing in a self-managed superannuation fund may be more expensive than investing in a retail fund. The key determinant will be the size of the fund.

Setting up a self-managed superannuation fund — some basic information

The following provides some very basic information on setting up a self-managed superannuation fund. If you are considering this option, it is very important that you discuss the most cost-effective structure with your broker or financial adviser before making a final decision. They can also advise you of any legislative changes current or pending that may affect you.

Start-up costs

Most of the costs associated with running an existing superannuation fund are tax deductible within the fund; however, the start-up costs for the funds are not deductible. You should be able to establish a standard one-to-four member fund for between $450 and $1,000.

Complying with the government's annual requirements usually costs around $600 to $1,500 per annum. This cost includes the ATO lodgment fee of around $50 a year.

These costs are indicative only. For a more exact estimate of the expenses involved, contact a professional adviser. Superannuation fund establishment fees are flat dollar amounts and not a percentage of assets as charged by other fund managers. If you currently have around $100,000 in the superannuation environment or can make substantial contributions to superannuation, you may seriously consider the self-managed superannuation option. With this much in superannuation, you could make significant savings on management fees through managing your own fund.

Superannuation members

There can be a minimum of one and a maximum of four members of a self-managed superannuation fund. Members are generally family or close business associates.

Trustee responsibilities

The trustee is responsible for investing and managing the assets of the fund in the best interests of the fund's members, and in accordance with the fund's trust deed and current legislation. Some obligations which trustees must observe are as follows:

- they must act honestly
- they must act in the interests of the members
- they must act within superannuation industry guidelines
- they must provide the required statutory returns.

Since 1 July 1999, the Australian Tax Office supervises the compliance of self-managed funds unless the trustees of the fund choose to nominate APRA to take on this role, in which case the fund is called an APRA fund.

Anyone can be appointed the trustee of a fund provided they are not an undischarged bankrupt and have not been convicted of an offence involving dishonesty. All members of self-managed funds must also be trustees of their fund.

Sourcing information about self-managed super funds

Some full-service brokers have client advisers who specialise in self-managed superannuation funds. The Financial Planning Association will be able to put you in touch with financial planners in your area.

Fact sheets and a list of publications relevant to setting up a self-managed superannuation fund can be sourced from the ATO's website (www.ato.gov.au).

The Australian Taxation Office, which supervises self-managed superannuation funds, provides a superannuation helpline on 13 10 20, a reasonable benefit limits helpline on 13 28 64 and a superannuation surcharge helpline on 13 10 20.

What can a self-managed fund invest in?

Trustees are relatively free to chart their own investment universe. Indeed, you can invest in literally anything you choose, provided it fits the fund's overall investment strategy, passes some basic tests and is within the legal guidelines. Questions to consider include:

- Is the investment part of the fund's investment strategy?
- What is the risk and return involved?
- How does it fit with overall diversification of assets?
- What is the fund's liquidity and ability to meet liabilities as they arise?
- Is the investment entered into and maintained on commercial terms?

Commercial terms

Commercial terms for superannuation funds means that the fund can demonstrate that market value has been paid and received on all transactions.

Who can contribute to a self-managed fund and when can they draw on benefits?

There are certain age-based rules relating to personal contributions to a superannuation fund. The rules as of July 2004 are explained below.

Under 65 years

Anyone under 65 can contribute to their superannuation fund, regardless of how much they are working.

65 to 75 years

If the member is between 65 and 75, contributions can only be made if the member has worked 40 hours in a 30-day period during the financial year in which the contributions will be made, but there are no tax deductions available once the member turns 70. After a member reaches the age of 65, he or she is subject to an annual work test, assessed on 1 July each year. Unless the member can prove that he or she worked 240 hours in the previous financial year, the member's total benefits must either be cashed or used to pay an income stream for the member.

More than 75 years

No further contributions may be accepted by a fund. At this age, no money can be left in the member's fund unless the member was already aged 75 on 1 July 2004 and is working more than 30 hours per week.

Eligible spouse contributions

Contributions for a low-income-earning spouse can be made up to the age of 70.

Once a member reaches the age of 65 and has retired, the fund must pay the benefit out either as a lump sum or as regular payments to the member. The latter is referred to as an income stream.

Establishing your own fund

Establishing your own fund is relatively straightforward, yet the golden rule is the same as that for all other aspects of investing: always seek professional advice. On the basis of this advice, you can get your self-managed fund up and running with confidence.

Step 1

To help you establish your self-managed superannuation fund, most professional advisers will prepare:

- the trust instrument
- the consent to act as a trustee
- the trustee minutes
- the tax file number application (as the fund requires its own tax file number)
- the Australian Business Number (ABN) application
- the notice of the election to become a regulated superannuation fund
- the membership application forms.

Members must also provide their tax file numbers.

Step 2

Once the fund is established, the trustees (you) open a bank account. A cash management trust with cheque and deposit book facilities is useful for this purpose.

Step 3

The trustees then determine and document an investment strategy to suit the needs of the members.

Step 4

The money can then be transferred into the fund and investments made accordingly.

Step 5

Once set up, you must maintain records for the fund. These include:

- contributions by members
- capital gains tax records
- income received
- capital transactions.

Of course, a professional adviser can assist in keeping these records and attend to all reports necessary to comply with taxation and reporting requirements.

Negative gearing

The term gearing refers to borrowing. When investors borrow, they are able to increase the amount of money they can invest, and with it their potential investment returns. When used astutely, gearing can be a very important wealth creation tool. Most loans require a form of security to be provided by the borrower to the lender.

Negative gearing occurs when money is borrowed to invest in an income producing asset and the income received from that asset is not sufficient to cover the interest payment on the monies borrowed — that is, the income is less than the interest expense. In some circumstances, the interest paid on borrowed funds is tax deductible.

The aim of any gearing exercise is to obtain a greater return by increasing the amount invested. This is known as leverage. Other terms include:

■ Neutral gearing, which occurs when money is borrowed to invest in an income-producing asset and the income received from that asset approximates the interest payment on the monies borrowed. In other words, the investment becomes self-funding.

- Positive gearing, which usually occurs when money is borrowed to invest in an income-producing asset and the income received from that asset exceeds the interest payment on the monies borrowed. Such investments are income positive.

Factors to consider

Risk

When you borrow, you increase the potential risk. There is an old saying 'the bigger the risk, the bigger the return'. However, as an investor, you should not gear unless you:

- understand the risk of your investment
- are prepared to accept the risk
- have the financial resources to meet the risk.

You must always look at the worst-case scenario and assess your ability to handle this situation if it occurs. If you borrow, you will be required at all times to:

- meet the loan repayment obligation
- maintain the loan within the agreed lending margin.

Where these requirements are breached, you may have to offer more security to the lender or reduce the loan to meet the agreed lending margin. Remember, negative gearing means you are making a loss and experiencing a negative cash flow. In order to meet your obligation, you may need to draw funds from other sources. Always consider your other sources of funds when you consider a negative gearing situation, as you will require secure regular income to meet the interest on the borrowing.

Security

When you borrow, the lender will usually require you to provide some security. The most common type of security requested by lenders is a mortgage over the income-producing asset. If you invest in shares, the mortgage is usually taken over those shares. A mortgage may also be taken over other assets such as non-related real estate or investments.

When you borrow, you should always ask the lender what percentage of the mortgaged asset they are prepared to lend against. This is known as the lending margin.

Lending margin

The proportion of the total investment a lender is prepared to advance for an investment in the sharemarket varies, but 35 per cent is about average. This means you may need to contribute 65 per cent in ready cash or shares already in your possession prior to borrowing the money.

Lenders have calculated lending margins for each share on the ASX. Each lender has the right to alter this margin if it changes its assessment of the company's prospects, and hence, the value of its shares. Most lenders allow the margin to fluctuate adversely by up to 5 per cent before requesting the investor to provide more security (a margin call) to ensure the percentage of the total investment made up of borrowed funds remains the same.

Figure 17.1, below, shows how a margin call works.

Margin lending

Margin lending is a loan from a stockbroker or another lender to purchase shares or units in managed funds. The loan is secured by the borrower's cash or shares (or other collateral) in addition to the shares or units purchased with the share money.

Figure 17.1: How a margin call works

$35k loan = 35%	$35k loan = 44%	$28k loan = 35%
		Margin call
$65k investor's capital = 65%	$45k investor's capital = 56%	+$45k investor's capital = 65%
Initial investment	Value of investment falls 20%	Margin call issued for $7,000
$100,000	$80,000	$80,000

There are three ways a margin call can be met:

1 further shares deposited (to increase the value of the portfolio) to be held as security for the loan (mortgage)

2 extra cash paid to reduce the loan

3 part of the portfolio sold to reduce the loan.

Borrowers can use one of these options or a combination of all three.

Borrowers usually have 24 hours to meet a margin call. Failure to meet a margin call may constitute a loan default, in which case the total amount owed becomes repayable immediately. Following a loan default on a margin call, the lender can sell the underlying shares without notifying the borrower.

Negative gearing — an example of the tax implications

To qualify for the tax concessions allowed when negative gearing is used, you must invest in an income-producing asset (or an asset that is likely to become income producing). This means the shares you buy must have a reasonable chance of earning dividends and should not be speculative stocks. If you invest in speculative shares with no prospect of dividends, you may not qualify for negative gearing in the opinion of the Australian Taxation Office.

An income-producing asset is said to be negatively geared where the amount of the deductions, including interest, is greater than the gross income received. In the case of shares, deductions are expenses you incur in gaining the dividend income. This loss on your investment in shares may be claimed as a deduction against other types of income such as salary and wages. Two of the most common types of negatively geared investments are real estate and shares.

In the example shown in Table 17.1, opposite, the dividend income received from the investment during the first year has imputation credits attached, which relate to the tax that has already been paid at the 30 per cent company tax rate. The imputation credits will appear on the investor's tax return as income, and be accompanied by a tax credit for the same amount.

As the loan used in the example is an interest-only loan, all outgoings are interest repayments.

Table 17.1 shows the tax implications and the after-tax cost of using negative gearing to leverage into shares. The calculations use 2004–2005 marginal tax rates.

Table 17.1: Fully (100%) geared share investment

Assumptions

Amount borrowed	$200,000
Interest rate	10% p.a.
Invested in shares with return of 5% (fully franked)	

Cash flows

Taxable personal income	$100,000
Dividend income received	$10,000
Imputation credits	$4,286
Loan interest	($20,000)
Net taxable income	$94,286
Tax on taxable income (see note 2)	$27,154
Net after-tax income	$67,132

Notes:

1. After-tax income before borrowing is $65,788.
2. Includes Medicare levy and franking credits.
3. The net cost in year one of gearing is $65,788 – $62,846 = $2,942 (with $62,846 being $67,132 less the imputed credit which is a non-cash item).

The following factors affect cash flow:

- level of dividends (dividend history)
- imputation credits (not received in cash)
- interest rate
- type of loan (repayments for principal and interest loans are higher than those for interest-only loans)
- borrowing costs (incurred in first year)
- margin calls.

Each of these factors should be taken into account when formulating your overall cash flow budget in a negative gearing proposal.

The example also assumes the investor takes the dividend in cash and does not participate in dividend reinvestment plans.

As mentioned earlier, always ensure that you have secure regular income in order to meet your negative gearing commitments. You should also have adequate insurance. Personal insurance cover is often said to lay a solid foundation for any investment portfolio.

With certain loans, you are able to prepay the interest for 12 months in advance.

Some loans also offer the opportunity for capitalising interest. In that case, the interest payment is added onto the loan balance (that is, the principal or capital owing). If this occurs, you have a large cash outflow initially and a larger tax loss. This loss can usually be offset against your income from other sources.

Critical steps to reducing risk while using negative gearing

The critical steps to reducing risk while using negative gearing are:

1   *Understand the effect of all fees such as establishment costs, ongoing charges and early repayment penalties by lending institutions.*

    Borrowing expenses are incurred in obtaining a loan to purchase income-producing shares. They may include such costs as establishment fees, valuation fees and fees for preparing mortgage documents. If the total of these costs is $100 or more, they are apportioned over five years, or the term of the loan, whichever is the lesser. If the total is less than $100, the fees are fully deductible in the year in which they were incurred.

Brokerage fees are incurred in the purchase of shares. They are generally of a capital nature and are therefore not tax deductible. As they relate to the purchase of the shares, they form part of the cost base. They do not form part of the income and expenditure statement.

2   *Use investments which produce regular income with some tax benefits.*

The shortfall or loss from negative gearing may be claimed as a deduction against other taxable income, thereby reducing your total tax payable. Depending on your type of income and your marginal rate of tax, this may lead to a refund of tax. This refund occurs after the end of the financial year and does not affect the cash flow in year one — that is, the tax benefit or refund will not occur until year two. The value of any tax benefit from negative gearing depends on individual circumstances and your marginal rate of tax. The higher your marginal rate of tax, the greater the tax benefit.

3   *Don't borrow more than you can afford to service, and always build in a safety margin.*

4   *Seek professional advice on the right strategy to employ: the choice of investments is critical.*

5   *Consider investment returns that are reasonably viable, particularly in a relatively low-inflation climate.*

Too often geared investments are entered into purely on a tax-driven basis, or on the promise of unsustainable past investment performance.

6   *Consider the investment program as long term (seven to ten years).*

7   *Select conservative equities and avoid using internally geared investments which increase your risks.*

8   *Ensure you continue to receive ongoing salary and interest income.*

Income-protection insurance should be considered.

Margin lenders

While some stockbroking firms do maintain in-house margin lending services, finance firms that specialise in equity lending include:

- BT Margin Lending   1800 816 222
- Challenger Margin Lending   1800 621 009
- Goldman Sachs JB Were   1300 366 790
- Leveraged Equities   1300 307 807
- Suncorp Margin Lending   13 11 55
- St George Margin Lending   1300 304 065

Taxation

This chapter provides share investors with an appreciation of the taxation implications and advantages associated with such investments. As always, you should seek advice on the tax implications before you engage in a share transaction.

Three areas of taxation affect share investors. They are:

1 capital gains tax (CGT) on the profit you make selling shares

2 income tax on any dividends you receive (which, under dividend imputation, is levied at your highest personal rate, minus any imputation credits)

3 taxation exemptions granted to employees receiving shares or share options at a discount under employee share schemes.

Taxation for share investors

This section provides an overview of the tax implications related to share investment.

Marginal tax rates

Table 18.1, overleaf, shows the 2004–2005 marginal tax rates for individuals.

Table 18.1: Individual tax rates 2004–2005

Taxable income	Marginal tax rate
$0–$6,000	0%
$6,001–$21,600	17%
$21,601–$58,000	30%
$58,001–$70,000	42%
Over $70,000	47%

Rates shown in Table 17.1 do not include the Medicare levy of 1.5 per cent. In addition, there is a 1 per cent Medicare surcharge for couples with combined income of $100,000 or more (and individuals with incomes of $50,000 or more) who do not take out private health cover. Low-income earners will be eligible to receive a tax rebate. The tax-free threshold is higher for certain taxpayers with dependent children.

Goods and services tax

A 10 per cent goods and services tax (GST) is payable on most types of goods or services supplied by a business for a payment (whether in cash or kind). To negate the inflationary effect and compensate consumers, the introduction of the GST was accompanied by:

- the removal of many state government taxes and levies (including the abolition of stamp duty on ASX share transactions from 1 July 2001)

- the removal of the Federal Wholesale Sales Tax (effective from 1 July 2000)

- personal income tax cuts.

Tax structures

The four basic tax structures are:

1   personal portfolio (single or jointly owned)

2   discretionary trust

3   private company

4   superannuation fund.

Before establishing a discretionary trust, a company or a private superannuation fund in which to hold your investments, you should consider the cost of doing so and the length of time the vehicle will be used. Such structures can cost up to $1,000 to implement and up to $1,000 a year to maintain. You should consult your adviser before you commit yourself to such a scheme.

Your personal portfolio

Your personal investment portfolio will benefit from the tax-free thresholds afforded to individuals. However, if you split that portfolio with another person — such as your husband, wife or partner — you may effectively reduce the tax rate applying to your portfolio if that person has a lower marginal tax rate. Investing personally can also secure a substantial CGT benefit. If you have held an investment or other asset for at least 12 months prior to disposing of it, only half of any capital gain arising from the disposal is subject to tax. Such gains are known as 'discounted capital gains'.

Capital gains tax is discussed in greater detail later in the chapter.

Discretionary trusts

Profits and dividends from investments held through a discretionary trust may be diverted to a variety of beneficiaries of the trust at the discretion of the trustee. Therefore, tax-averaging strategies can be put in place, especially when there is one major taxpayer investing with several lesser taxpayers.

Private companies

People paying a high personal tax rate (48.5 per cent, including Medicare levy) may consider operating through a private company tax structure. While trusts are required to pay tax at the maximum marginal tax rate in respect to realised profits and income which is not distributed to beneficiaries, companies are not, meaning investment portfolios could be developed over a long period of time. This strategy was particularly useful for deferring the payment of tax to a time more suitable to the taxpayer.

However, given the 50 per cent discount for capital gains on assets held by individuals for 12 months or more, the effective tax rate on capital gains may be 24.25 per cent (being somewhat lower than the corporate tax rate of 30 per cent). Accordingly, depending upon your investment profile, a corporate structure may be less efficient.

You should consider obtaining professional advice before investing through a corporate structure.

Superannuation funds

Superannuation funds are a particularly attractive means of accumulating assets in a tax-efficient manner. Income generated within a super fund is taxed at 15 per cent, as are the tax deductible contributions made to the fund. Capital gains made by a superannuation fund are taxed at a rate of 10 per cent if the relevant investments were held for 12 or more months, or 15 per cent if they were held for less than a year.

Therefore, for an individual with an average tax rate of greater than 15 per cent, it may be advisable to accumulate an asset within a superannuation vehicle, provided the investor fully understands the restrictions on withdrawing funds from the superannuation environment.

Don't forget that you do not necessarily have to claim a tax deduction for the contributions that you make to your superannuation fund. Higher income earners become liable for the superannuation surcharge tax. This is applied to the 'surchargable contributions', which include deductible member and all employer contributions. This may mean that it is not appropriate to claim a deduction.

Franking credits earned by complying super funds can be used to:

- offset tax on internal earnings
- offset net realised capital gains within the fund
- offset tax on the contributions to the fund.

Excess franking credits received by a complying super fund are refundable.

Annuities and allocated pensions

You may elect to receive money from your superannuation fund in the form of an annuity or allocated pension. There are many types of annuities but all have one feature in common — the use of capital to purchase a regular income stream which may be paid monthly, quarterly, six-monthly or annually. An annuity may only be offered by a life company, friendly society, trade union fund or a complying pension.

The annuitant may elect to have any selected percentage of the original annuity purchase price returned at the end of the annuity term, ranging from zero to 100 per cent residual capital value.

The term of the annuity may also be selected by the purchaser and can range from one year up to a maximum number of years equal to the actuarial life expectancy of the purchaser. The annuity may also be for life (however long that may be), or even have an income which reverts to a surviving partner upon death of the original purchaser. The capital in a lifetime annuity is not available to any beneficiaries of an estate and the income can only go to a reversionary annuitant.

You can elect to have annuity income indexed to a set percentage each year, or to CPI. Be aware that many CPI-indexed annuity incomes may have an indexation ceiling, limiting income growth in any one year.

In the case of allocated pensions, unlike a lifetime annuity, the capital is available to beneficiaries of the estate, they have no set term and they last as long as the capital invested lasts. Furthermore, the capital can be accessed at any time. The government sets the minimum and maximum pensions that can be taken out each year and this is dependent on your age and is a proportion of your capital.

The tax advantages of an annuity/allocated pension are fourfold:

1   Annuity/allocated pension funds are not subject to income or capital gains tax — they are taxed in the hands of the recipient.

2   If the money used to buy an annuity/allocated pension is rolled over from a superannuation fund, the income will attract a personal tax rebate for the annuitant equal to 15 per cent of the rebatable income.

3   The voluntary (undeducted contributions) will be progressively paid out over the term of the annuity/ allocated pension as tax-free income, otherwise known as deductible income. In an annuity, an election to receive some of the capital at the end of the annuity term (this is not a lifetime annuity) will reduce the tax-free income.

4   There is a 15 per cent rebate on the balance of the income stream.

Dividend imputation

Dividend imputation refers to the system whereby companies paying tax in Australia distribute dividends with tax rebates attached. These dividends are known as franked dividends.

The tax paid by companies is attributed (imputed) to the dividends distributed to shareholders. The purpose of attribution (or imputation) is to relieve the shareholder of some or all of the tax otherwise payable on the distribution, thereby preventing the double taxation of company profits.

Since 1 July 1987, taxation under the imputation system has applied to dividends paid to Australian resident shareholders by:

- Australian companies
- corporate unit trusts
- public trading trusts.

Franked dividends are those dividends paid out of an Australian-based company's after-tax income, as shown in Figure 18.1, below. The Australian company tax rate at the time of writing is 30 per cent.

Figure 18.1: Source of franked dividends

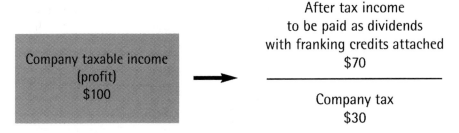

When a company pays income tax, the procedure gives rise to franking credits. Figure 18.1 shows how franking credits accrue when a company pays tax on its taxable income (profit) that is paid out as dividends.

Tax on company profit resulting in franking credits

If you receive a franked dividend and are an Australian resident, you will be entitled to claim an imputation credit — provided you satisfy the 'holding period rule' in respect of the shares. The holding period requires that you own the shares without a reduced risk of gains or losses from those shares (through hedging or other means) for 45 days. The holding period may be satisfied at any point from the day after the date of acquisition and the number of days in the holding period after the shares go ex dividend.

An exemption to the holding period rule will apply to all individuals with a total franking rebate of $5,000 or less.

Some listed companies pay a proportion of both franked and unfranked dividends. Therefore, the total dividend you receive from a company may be 'partly franked' — that is, made up of both franked and unfranked portions.

If a dividend is fully franked, it will be substantially tax-free in the hands of an individual shareholder. However, if an investor is paying personal income tax at the highest marginal rate, they will be required to pay tax at a rate equal to the difference between that rate and the company tax rate of 30 per cent.

Examples of the use of franked dividends

The following examples show the effect of the different marginal tax rates on income earned and include the 1.5 per cent Medicare levy. The example in Table 18.2, below, shows the different treatment of interest income and dividend income.

Table 18.2: Franked dividends vs interest income

	Taxpayer A $	Taxpayer B $
Salary	30,000	30,000
Dividend income (franked)	7,000	–
Interest income	–	7,000
Sub-total	37,000	37,000
Imputation credits	3,000	–
Taxable income	40,000	37,000
Tax payable (includes Medicare levy)	8,980	8,035
Less franking credits	(3,000)	–
Net tax payable	5,980	8,035
Overall average tax rate	14.95%	21.7%

The overall average rate of tax expressed as a percentage of taxable income is less for Taxpayer A, who receives franked dividends, than Taxpayer B, who receives interest. This is due to the effect of the imputation credits and the taxpayer's marginal tax rate.

The value of the franking credits to shareholders depends on their marginal tax rate. When your marginal tax rate is higher than the 30 per cent already paid by the company, you will be required to pay extra income tax to make up the difference. Where your marginal tax rate is 30 per cent or less, you effectively pay no tax on dividends received. As mentioned, any excess franking credits can be applied to reduce the tax otherwise payable on other sources of income or, if there is no such tax otherwise payable, you can obtain a cash refund for the excess franking credits.

Table 18.3, below, shows the excess rebate available from $70 franked dividends, for each marginal tax rates.

Table 18.3: Franking rebates for each marginal tax rate

Company level	$			
Taxable income	100			
Company tax (30%)	30			
After-tax income (paid as dividend)	70			
Shareholder level	47% Tax $	42% Tax $	30% Tax $	17% Tax $
Dividend received	70	70	70	70
Imputation credits	30	30	30	30
Assessable income	100	100	100	100
Tax assessed	47	42	30	17
Less franking rebate	(30)	(30)	(30)	(30)
Tax payable	17	12	Nil	Nil
Excess rebate to offset tax on other Income	Nil	Nil	Nil	17

The table details the implications of receiving a dividend in the hands of four different taxpayers. All taxpayers need to declare in their income tax returns the 'grossed-up dividend'. This is equal to the actual dividend received, plus the imputation or tax credits received. The Medicare levy is ignored in the calculations shown in Table 18.3.

Imputation credits and different investment vehicles

Imputation credits may pass through:

■ chains of resident companies who are shareholders (and affect the franking accounts) where the relevant dividends are fully franked, and through wholly owned groups of companies where the relevant dividends are not fully franked

■ trusts and partnerships to individual persons.

Partnerships

A partnership result for the 2004–2005 year may be as shown below.

Dividend income	$10,000 (includes imputation credits of $3,000; franked dividends of $7,000)
Other income	($30,000)
Net loss	($20,000)

A partner who has a 50 per cent interest in the partnership would include $10,000 as a loss distribution, with $1,500 also being distributed as franking credits available to be offset against the partner's other income.

As you can see from this example, the most appropriate investment vehicle depends on a person's individual circumstances. To determine your position, speak to your investment adviser or accountant.

What is capital gains tax?

Capital gains tax (CGT) generally applies to assets, including shares, acquired on or after 20 September 1985. A capital gain arises where the net proceeds on the sale of an asset exceeds its cost base (indexation may apply — see below). In the case of shares, the cost base comprises the share purchase price plus incidental costs of acquisition such as brokers' fees. CGT is payable at your marginal tax rate in the year in which you sell the shares. This may be lower than your current marginal tax rate if, for example, you sell the shares when you have retired and are earning less income. A reduced CGT rate applies to assets owned by individuals that are held for at least twelve months before disposal. Only half of the capital gain arising from the sale of such assets is subject to tax. Gains taxed at the reduced rate are known as 'discounted capital gains'. One of the advantages of investing in shares for capital growth is that you do not have to pay tax on the higher value of your shares until you actually sell them for a profit.

Whenever individual taxpayers derive a net capital gain, they are required to include that gain in their assessable income for the period during which it arose. Net capital losses (that is, where the cost base exceeds net proceeds) can only be offset against capital gains. The taxpayer is entitled to carry forward any unused capital losses to offset future capital gains. In limited circumstances (that is, for assets acquired before 21 September 1999), you may still apply indexation to the cost base of the asset but if you do, you cannot take advantage of discounted capital gains.

Calculation of CGT

The calculation of capital gains tax, depending on when the asset was purchased and how long it has been held for, is shown in Table 18.4, overleaf.

Table 18.4: Calculation of capital gains tax

Date Purchased	Held for 12 Months or more	Held for less than 12 months
pre 21 September 1999	100% of indexed gain (proceeds minus indexed cost base at 30 September 1999) or 50% of actual gain (proceeds minus cost) assessable	100% of actual gain (proceeds minus cost) assessable
post 21 September 1999	50% of actual gain (proceeds minus cost) assessable	100% of actual gain

It will generally only be worthwhile to choose to index capital gains, rather than obtain discounted capital gains, where the asset disposed of was acquired before April 1987.

As an investor, it is essential that you maintain good records. You must keep full details for each quantity of shares you purchase, thereby enabling the accurate calculation of the appropriate capital gain or loss on disposal, and must retain records for five years after the CGT event (such as the disposal of shares).

The capital gain (or discounted capital gain) is included in the taxpayer's assessable income and tax is calculated in the same manner as tax on any other type of income.

CGT calculations

The following example shown in Table 18.5, opposite, details the CGT payable on the disposal of a hypothetical parcel of shares by an individual. In this instance, the assessable capital gain is $905.95 (being 50 per cent of $1,811.90). Like all capital gains, it is taxed at the person's marginal rate of tax. If that person is in the highest tax bracket, the gain is taxed at 47 per cent. Capital gains are not included in your 'instalment income' for the purpose of the pay-as-you-go (PAYG) instalment system.

Table 18.5: Capital gain on disposal of shares (using base data)

Stock	Date of shares	Number per share	Price amount*	Total
Acquisition: Parcel 1 XYZ	30/10/1999	715	$3.55	$2,538.25
Disposal: Parcel 1 XYZ	27/12/2000	715	$6.21	$4,440.15

Less commission on disposal: ($90.00)
Net proceeds: $4,350.15
*Acquisition price per share includes all costs.

Calculation of capital gain

Net proceeds on disposal: $4,350.15
Cost base: $2,538.25 (as the shares were acquired after 21 September 1999, no indexation is available)
Capital gain: $1,811.90
Discounted capital gain: $905.95 (subject to tax)

CGT and different asset types

Share investments usually deal with the following assets:

- ordinary shares
- preference shares
- bonus shares
- convertible notes
- rights to acquire shares (options)
- options to acquire unissued shares.

Some of the major features of bonus shares, convertible notes, and rights or options to acquire shares relative to the CGT legislation are discussed below.

Bonus shares

The cost base for bonus shares is the cost base of the original existing shares. It is determined by spreading the sum of any amounts paid for all those shares across the original existing shares and the bonus shares. The acquisition is the date of acquisition of the original shares.

Where the bonus shares do not represent a dividend and the original shares were acquired before 20 September 1985, the bonus shares are deemed to be pre-CGT shares.

Convertible notes

In the case of acquisition of convertible notes before 20 September 1985, there are two scenarios:

1   If the convertible notes were acquired before 20 September 1985 and no further monies are payable on conversion to shares, the shares will retain their pre-CGT status and the subsequent sale of the shares will be CGT exempt.

2   If the convertible notes were acquired before 20 September 1985 and further monies are payable on conversion to shares, the shares will be deemed to have been acquired on the date of the conversion. Accordingly, the shares will lose the pre-CGT status. For CGT purposes, the cost base will be the market value of the convertible notes when the conversion took place, plus any further conversion monies paid.

Where the convertible notes are acquired after 20 September 1985, the acquisition cost of the notes plus any further payments will be the cost base on conversion of the notes to shares. The shares are deemed to be acquired when the convertible note was acquired.

Rights or options to acquire shares

Where rights or options are issued to a shareholder by a company for no consideration, the rights or options are deemed to have been acquired by the shareholder at the date the existing shares were acquired. The exercising of such rights is not a disposal for CGT purposes.

Where rights are issued to a shareholder by a company for a consideration, the acquisition date (of the rights) is the date that the shareholder paid the money for the rights regardless of the date the existing shares were acquired.

For more information, contact your local branch of the Australian Taxation Office and request a copy of its *Guide to Capital Gains Tax*. Alternatively, you can telephone the ATO (1300 364 365) or visit its website (www.ato.gov.au).

Other areas for consideration

Employee share schemes

An employee share scheme is an arrangement whereby employees of a particular company (usually a listed company) are entitled to take up ownership in the form of shares. Generally, any discount from the market price of the shares is to be included in the assessable income of the employee. However, shares issued under such an arrangement may attract certain concessional taxation treatment which acts to either defer the point in time at which any discount is assessed, or to reduce the amount to be assessed. For example, employees are entitled to receive a discount up to $1,000 from the market price of the shares tax-free provided certain conditions are met. These conditions include the following:

- there is not potential for an employee to forfeit ownership of the shares

- restrictions as to disposal of shares issued under such a scheme exist

- the scheme is offered to permanent employees of the company on a non-discriminatory basis.

Dividend reinvestment

Dividends reinvested in further shares are taxed in exactly the same manner as dividends received in cash. All details noted on the advice you receive from the company must be included on your income tax return. When you receive a dividend in cash only one transaction occurs. Dividend reinvestment plans generate two transactions:

1   the receipt of a dividend

2   the purchase of shares.

The tax aspects of the purchase of shares are covered in the capital gains tax section of this chapter.

Property trusts

Both listed and unlisted property trusts can in some circumstances distribute some of their income as tax-deferred income (tax can be deferred until the recipient sells the investment). These tax benefits reflect depreciation allowances provided to the building owners and passed onto investors in the trusts. As a result, it is possible that only part of the distribution will be taxable in the hands of the investor. This results in a downward adjustment to the cost base of units held by investors and increases their capital gains liability at the time of sale.

Taxing traders vs taxing investors

Under capital gains tax legislation, traders and investors are treated differently. All returns made by traders on the sale of shares will be treated as a trading profit, in the same way as the profits of a corner shop selling groceries. Likewise, trading losses are fully deductible — unlike capital losses, which can only be offset against capital gains. An investor's profits on the sale of the shares will be treated as a capital profit and is subject to capital gains tax.

A potential taxation benefit to share traders is that, via the valuation of the shares on hand at June 30 (that is, at market or cost value), any unrealised losses will be able to be brought to account. A major disadvantage will be that the 50 per cent discount available for assets held for 12 months or more will not apply, and all profits will be fully taxable.

The test of whether a taxpayer is a share trader or an investor is both subjective and objective, but is essentially one of fact. In deciding this issue, case law has established the following to be the most relevant considerations:

- the repetition and regularity in the buying and selling of shares
- the number and volume of share transactions
- whether the taxpayer is operating to a plan, setting budgets and targets, and keeping records
- whether the taxpayer maintains an office
- whether the taxpayer accounts for the share transactions on a gross receipts basis
- whether the taxpayer is engaged in another full-time profession.

Your accountant will be able to assist you in determining whether you are a share trader or an investor.

Glossary

allocated pension A pension arrangement, similar to an annuity, where a person has their own account and regularly draws down an amount from the account, within certain legislated limits. The pension continues till death or until the account is exhausted. An allocated pension is different to a traditional pension in that it offers continual access to the capital sum invested, flexibility in draw-downs and no protection against money running out early.

All Ordinaries (All Ords) This index measures the level of share prices at any given time for approximately 500 of the largest Australian companies to determine the overall performance of the sharemarket. The index was established by the ASX at 500 points in January 1980. The companies are weighted according to their size in terms of market capitalisation (total market value of a company's shares).

All Ordinaries Accumulation Index This index lists the same companies as the All Ords but also takes into account capital appreciation and dividends in calculating returns.

annual report In the context of the Australian sharemarket, the annual report is a financial report or statement issued by a publicly listed company to its shareholders. The annual report contains a statement of financial performance, a statement of financial position, a statement of cash flow, as well as notice of the Annual General Meeting (AGM) and business resolutions to be discussed.

annuity A series of identical fixed payments to be made for a specified number of years.

ASIC (Australian Securities and Investments Commission) The government body responsible for (among other things) regulating companies, the issue and sale of shares and trust units, company borrowings, and investment advisers and dealers, in accordance with the *Corporations Act 2001 (Cth)*.

asset allocation The proportion of your total capital you invest in the different asset classes. This will be largely determined by your risk profile.

at limit An order that places a limit on either the highest price that may be paid for shares or the lowest price that may be accepted for sale.

at market An order that is placed at a price where the bid equals the best opposing offer, or the offer equals the best opposing bid.

bear market A market where share prices are falling quite sharply and experts expect further falls.

bid The price at which someone is prepared to buy shares (opposite to offer).

blue chip Shares, usually highly valued, in a major company known for its ability to make profits in good times or in bad, with reduced risk of default.

bonus shares/bonus issue Additional shares issued by the company to existing shareholders for free, usually in a pre-determined ratio to the number of shares already held.

books closing date The date at which a company's share register is closed off to identify the shareholders and to calculate any entitlement to new issues and dividends.

bottom-up approach Investment process of selecting shares looking at individual companies — their outlook, what they do and their financial information.

brokerage Fee paid to stockbroking firm for buying or selling of shares.

bull market A market where share prices are generally rising.

business cycle Also known as the economic cycle. The rise and fall of the economy, from a peak, or boom, to a trough (sometimes called a depression) and back to a peak. The length and duration of each phase is not predictable.

capital Funding for investment in capital assets or to operate a business. Also refers to the value of an investment in a business or in assets such as property or shares.

capital growth An increase in the value in an asset such as of an investment in shares. Capital growth is realised as a capital gain when the asset is sold for more than its purchase price.

cash management trust A fixed interest trust designed specifically for short-term investors. This means entry and exit fees are not normally charged. Interest usually accrues on a daily basis at a variable rate related to the actual earning rate each day.

CHESS The ASX's Clearing House Electronic Sub-Register System which provides the central register for electronic transfer of share ownership.

company report Under *Corporations Act 2001 (Cth)*, a listed company must provide a range of reports. These include half yearly reports, preliminary final reports as well as annual reports.

contract note A written document confirming a transaction between two dealers or a broker and a client which details the costs, type and quantity of shares traded.

contrarian investors Investors who invest against the general tide and sentiments of the market.

contributing shares Shares that have been partly paid for. At a future date the shareholder will be required to pay the balance outstanding, unless the company is a no liability company in which case shares can be forfeited instead.

convertible note A loan made to a company at a fixed rate of interest with the right to be either redeemed (that is, repaid by the company) for cash or converted into ordinary shares at a predetermined date or within a certain period.

cum dividend Cum means 'with'. Shares quoted cum dividend entitle the buyer to the current dividend. The price of the shares will usually reflect the amount of the dividend. Similarly, shares 'cum rights' enable the buyer to participate in the new issue of shares.

cyclicals Businesses that are reliant on the general economy for growth and have little intrinsic protection against soft periods.

debenture A loan to a company at a fixed rate of interest and for a fixed term, usually one to five years. The debenture is secured by a trust deed over an asset, or assets, of a company.

derivatives Derivatives are instruments that derive their value from that of underlying instruments (such as shares, share price indices, fixed-interest securities, commodities and currencies). Warrants and exchange traded options are types of derivatives.

diversification Spreading investments over a variety of investment categories in order to reduce risk. You may also invest in different countries to spread your risk.

dividend Distribution of part of a company's net profit to shareholders. Usually expressed as a number of cents per share.

dividend cover A ratio showing the number of times a company's dividend is covered by its net profit. Dividend cover ratio equals net profit divided by total dividend paid. A low dividend cover points to a company paying out most of their net profit, while a high cover suggests much of the profit is being retained.

dividend imputation The tax credits passed onto a shareholder who receives a franked dividend. Under provisions of the *Income Tax Assessment Act*, imputation credits entitle investors to a rebate for tax already paid by an Australian company.

dividend per share (DPS) Represents the cash payment or distribution made by a company to shareholders on a per share basis. The payment is made out of the earnings of the company. Calculated by adding the interim dividend to the final dividend, DPS is usually expressed as cents per share.

dividend yield The annual dividend shown as a percentage of the last sale price for the shares. A simplified rate of return on an investment.

earnings cycle Graphical analysis method used to explain reflexivity in markets — that is, that markets are always biased in one direction or the other and that markets can influence the events they anticipate.

earnings per share (EPS) Measures the earnings that are attributed to each equivalent ordinary share over a twelve-month period. It is calculated by dividing the company's earnings by the number of shares on issue.

equity capital or equity funding Capital raised by a company through issuing shares. An alternative to debt funding.

ex-date The date at which a previously announced dividend or issue is deemed to take place. It is usually five business days before a company's 'books closing date'. If you purchase shares after the ex-date, you will not be entitled to the current new issue of shares or the dividend.

ex dividend Shares sold ex dividend entitle the seller to retain the current dividend. Shares are usually quoted ex dividend five business days before the company's books close.

fixed assets Assets which are not easily converted into cash such as your house or superannuation.

float The initial raising of capital by public subscription to securities, such as shares offered on the sharemarket for the first time.

franked dividend A dividend paid by a company out of profits on which the company has already paid tax. The investor is entitled to an imputation credit, or reduction in the amount of income tax that must be paid, up to the amount of tax already paid by the company.

fundamental analysis Method of analysis using ratios and percentages calculated from financial data of a company to assess the company's quantitative and qualitative aspects. Ratios of particular industry groups and/or major competitors may also be included in the analysis to determine it's suitability for investment.

general market risk The risk of volatility within the market as a whole or within a particular sector of the market — for example, mining shares are usually more volatile than bank shares.

goods and services tax (GST) A broad-based tax of 10 per cent on most supplies of goods and services consumed in Australia. On July 2000 the GST replaced wholesale sales tax.

government bond A debt security issued by the government. Interest is usually paid twice yearly at a fixed rate for the life of the bond, which is usually 10 years.

growth companies Companies which have already achieved above average earnings growth and are expected to continue doing so.

holder identification number (HIN) Allocated by your stockbroking firm when you buy shares if you nominate them as your sponsor in CHESS.

income An investor's income includes dividends, interest and other payments received from investments. It does not include capital growth.

Interest Rate Market (IRM) The ASX market where it is possible to buy and sell interest rate products, such as corporate bonds, floating rate notes, convertible notes and hybrid securities.

intuitive models Analysis methods, partially based on economic conditions, that mostly use subjective inputs from the investor and rely on his or her understanding of how markets work.

investment clock Analysis tool which sets out simply the economic and investment cycles using the analogy of a sweeping hour hand to pass through various economic stages or cycles.

liquid assets Assets which you can easily convert into cash, such as shares or fixed-interest investments.

liquidity Being able to convert assets into cash easily, quickly and with little or no loss of capital. A liquid market is a market with enough participants to make buying and selling easy.

listed company A company which has agreed to abide by ASX listing rules so that its shares can be bought and sold on the ASX.

macro-economic models Analysis methods which use economic data as inputs to forecast market movements.

margin call Occurs when the amount borrowed to invest in shares exceeds the lending margin. For example, a company agrees to lend money using shares as collateral to the value of 70 per cent of the shares. If the share price falls, the amount borrowed rises above 70 per cent and the borrower will be required to provide extra funds to bring the loan amount back to 70 per cent of the collateral.

market capitalisation The total number of shares on issue multiplied by their market price. This can be applied to work out the market value of one company or of the value of all companies listed on the exchange.

market price The prevailing price of shares traded on the ASX. It may be the last price at which the shares traded, or the most recent price offered or bid for the shares.

negative gearing Negative gearing is a situation in which you borrow money to invest in an income-producing asset and the income received from that asset is less than the interest expense. The interest expense on borrowed funds may be tax deductible.

net tangible assets (NTA) An indication of what each share in a company is worth if all the assets were liquidated, all the debts were paid and the residual was distributed to the ordinary shareholders on a per share basis.

offer The price at which someone is prepared to sell shares (opposite to bid).

off-market transfer The transfer of shares between parties without using a stockbroking firm as the intermediary. Off-market transfers are executed through the use of an Australian Standard Transfer Form.

ordinary shares The most commonly traded security in Australia. Holders of ordinary shares are part owners of a company and may receive payments in cash, called dividends, if the company trades profitably. A class of shares which have no preferential rights to either dividends out of profits or capital on a winding up.

Porter 'five forces' framework A useful tool used for analysing the outlook for a particular industry sector. There are five underlying factors according to this framework which determine future profitability — power of suppliers, power of customers, risk of new entrants, risk of substitute products and degree of rivalry in industry.

preference shares Shares that rank before ordinary shares in the event of liquidation of the issuing company and that usually receive a fixed rate of return.

price/earnings ratio Shows the number of times the price covers the earnings per share over a twelve-month period. Investors commonly use this ratio to measure the attractiveness of particular shares and to compare shares in one company with those in another.

price range for day The highest and lowest price at which a share traded over the course of a day.

prospectus The document issued by a company or fund setting out the terms of its public equity issue or debt raising. This provides the background, and financial and management status of the company or fund, subject to the requirements of ASX listing rules and the *Corporations Act 2001 (Cth)*.

return/return on investment What you earn from your investments, including dividends, interest or other income and realised capital gains. Return is usually expressed as a percentage of the amount invested.

rights issue A privilege granted to shareholders to buy new shares in the same company, usually below the prevailing market price.

risk profile Your attitude to risk, determined by a range of factors including your stage of life, the amount you have to invest, your experience and confidence as well as your investment time frame.

S&P/ASX indices Measure the movement in share values resulting from trading on the ASX. The indices are constructed and calculated by Standard & Poors.

SEATS The Stock Exchange's Automated Trading System. It provides for the trading of securities on the ASX.

securities A general term applied to all shares, debentures, notes, bills, government and semi-government bonds.

security-holder reference number (SRN) This is allocated by an issuer to identify a holder on an issuer sponsored or certificated subregister.

self-managed superannuation fund A privately run superannuation fund of between one and four members. It is established via a trust instrument that sets out how each fund is to operate and who the members and trustees are.

shares Shares represent part-ownership in a company. They can be ordinary shares, preference shares or partly-paid (contributing) shares.

small-capitalisation shares Also called 'small-cap' stocks, these are the smaller companies outside the top 500.

specific risk The risk of a particular share underperforming the market.

stockbroker A stockbroker has direct access to the market for trading shares. Therefore, he or she can act as your agent to buy or sell shares, for which a fee is charged. A broker may also offer a range of other products and services including providing advice on which shares to buy or sell.

SWOT analysis Process used to analyse a company's strengths, weaknesses, opportunities and threats.

technical analysis Method used to identify investment opportunities through the study of price action. A chart, representing past price movements, is the principal tool used to identify trends on which analysts can base their future predictions.

top-down approach An investment philosophy which looks firstly at the social, economic and political forces which may affect the nature and shape of the economic cycle. From these theoretical positions, analysts examine and interpret market forecasts to develop a picture of the investment environment which helps to determine whether the investment strategy should be bullish, bearish or neutral.

underwriter Guarantees to the company that the funds sought — through a float, for example — will be raised, that any shortfall will be taken up by the underwriter and that the funds will be available at a specific time.

unsecured notes A loan made to a company for a fixed period of time at a fixed rate of interest. They are issued mainly, but not only, by finance companies for between three months and three years. They offer a higher rate of interest than a debenture of the same maturity, but do not have the same security as a debenture.

volatility Measure of the amount of fluctuation in price of the underlying security calculated using the standard deviation of average daily price change.

warrants Financial instruments issued by a bank or other financial institutions, that are traded on ASX's equity market. Warrants may be issued over securities such as shares in a company, a currency, an index or a commodity.

Index